# Winning Ways for MINISTERS' WIVES

## Shirley E. Montgomery

**BROADMAN PRESS**

Nashville, Tennessee

© Copyright 1987 • Broadman Press
All rights reserved
4227-10
ISBN: 0-8054-2710-4

Dewey Decimal Classification: 253.2
Subject Heading: MINISTERS' WIVES
Library of Congress Catalog Card Number: 87-8050
Printed in the United States of America

Scripture quotations are taken from the *Good News Bible,* the Bible in Today's English Version. Old Testament: Copyright © American Bible Society 1976; New Testament: Copyright © American Bible Society 1966, 1971, 1976. Used by permission.

**Library of Congress Cataloging-in-Publication Data**

Montgomery, Shirley E.
    Winning ways for ministers' wives.

    1. Clergymen's wives.   I. Title.
BV4395.M584    1987        253'.2        87-8050
ISBN 0-8054-2710-4 (pbk.)

To

my parents

**William E. and Lula Shirrell Ennis**

and

these churches I served as a pastor's wife

Muldraugh Baptist Church
Muldraugh, Kentucky

First Baptist Church
Clay, Kentucky

South Avondale Baptist Church
Birmingham, Alabama

Lakeview Baptist Church
Auburn, Alabama

# Contents

# Up Front and Personal

Thank you for giving me your fellowship through this book. It is always a joy to find someone who shares my concern about ministers' wives.

Three aims came to mind in writing this book: (1) setting down some helpful hints for new ministers' wives, (2) encouraging those who've been in their role for a while, and (3) celebrating the wisdom and gifts of those who've spent a lifetime in this special role. Wherever you are on your pilgrimage, I hope you can find hope, comfort, insight, or even a chuckle of recognition in these pages.

The call to ministry is a mixed blessing. Being where God wants us to be is a great feeling. Getting there and staying there, however, can sometimes be a real hassle! This book is designed to help ministers' wives tilt the scales toward the positive, winning side of ministry. Each chapter deals with concerns often voiced by ministers' wives at seminars and retreats. Explanations, practical guidelines, and encouragement about expectations, role identity, family life enrichment, relationships, stress, ministerial rough spots, and personal growth are spotlighted.

As a minister's wife for over twenty-five years, I've been in and out of most of the areas of concern. I think I've grown from the experience. Other ministers' wives have shared their pilgrimage with me, and their insights are part of this book also. Add your experience to the process, and we'll all grow together—understanding, accepting, and celebrating our role as God leads us.

SHIRLEY MONTGOMERY
NASHVILLE, TENNESSEE

Now let me introduce you to *Joan and Todd*. They are minister's wife and minister, a fictional pair, and a composite of many actual couples. But I've met the Joans out there, and I think you have too. I'll let her introduce each chapter in her own unique way.

*Here's Joan . . .*

# 1

# Seeing the Big Picture

*Joan sat on the steps of the married students' apartments at seminary. She and her husband Todd had just moved in. This place would probably be their home for the next three years or so. What a shock! Joan thought their future lay in Todd's career in the army. Now he was studying for the ministry. Joan felt isolated and a little afraid. She had not been all that active in church before. "What will it be like," Joan wondered, "and what will people expect of me? I can't believe I'm going to be a minister's wife."*

Welcome to the title of *minister's wife!* It's part of your identity now. Those two words hold a world of different meanings for you and for those around you. The title makes a quick introduction to your place in the community. It also makes a handy peg on which to hang a lot of preconceived ideas and expectations of you as a minister's wife.

What do churches and church members expect of you as a minister's wife? That question is not easy to answer. There are probably some basic points of agreement, but you'd have to ask each church and each person to get the whole picture!

In practical terms, however, there are some general ideas about ministry that influence most people's thinking. Also, church members probably know what they liked or disliked about clergy wives they've known in the past. They likely have a mental picture of what a minister's wife should look like and what she should do. Churches and clergy wives tend to tolerate each other, sometimes winding up happy with each other and sometimes not. Reasons for their feelings are not easy to pinpoint, and often any number of issues are tied up in either good or unpleasant relationships between them.

Shouldn't there be a better way of getting to know and accept each other as clergy wife and congregation? Of course! And you can learn some skills to help the process along. You can benefit by finding out what the church or other service organization wants of you as a minister's wife. By nailing down some specific expectations, you can make a smoother entry into the group and understand better how your own needs can be met in the relationship.

To help you get started, let's look at some common ideas about ministry held by the general public. From these ideas we'll move to some expectations often expressed by churches as they seek ministers to serve with them. You can get some grasp of your role expectations by looking at these ideas.

## Common Ideas About Ministry

Have you ever been told, "You just don't look like a minister's wife," or some similar statement? What the person meant is that you didn't match his or her mental picture of a clergy wife. The temptation is to ask: "Just what should a minister's wife look like? Is there a standard model?" The question would be funny if it were not so tied up in very real attitudes toward you and your role.

Some ideas about ministers and their families are practical and some pure fantasy. Ideas grow out of past experience in the church, friendships with a certain clergy family, or sometimes from gossip in the local community. Stereotypes of ministers and their wives show up in novels, TV, or movies. Together these concepts help form a popular image of clergy couples. How true this image may be depends on the source of information. No matter how farfetched these ideas about ministry may be, they do have an effect on how you may be accepted by some people.

Let's look at some very broad ideas about ministry as a background to locating specific expectations. Note that the role concepts focus primarily on the minister. These ideas, however, do carry over to ministers' wives as well, and we'll apply that connection later on. Right now it's important to get in mind the mental image many people have as they relate to your husband.

Three role concepts can be used to sum up popular thinking about the clergy: (1) ministers serve as *symbols;* (2) ministers serve as helpers, often as *heroic figures;* and (3) ministers serve as *examples.* Why are these ideas important to you? Simply because many individuals and churches look on the minister and his wife as a team, some seeing them as two halves of the same identity.

### Symbolic Role

Answering God's call through commitment to a vocation in ministry naturally tags some people as different or sets them apart in the church. They fill a special place in the community of faith. As ministers these persons are expected to give leadership, spiritual guidance, and insight into God's Word. Therefore it is no wonder that the clergy are usually seen as God's representatives inside and outside the church.

People tend to relate in a different kind of way to anyone who claims the role of *minister.* Personal doubts, anxieties, guilt feelings, and religious hopes often come to rest on the minister. Some persons actually look on ministers as stand-ins for God. In fact, their concept of God may be based on what they see in a minister. So ministry often raises some deep-seated feelings in people that affect their attitudes about the clergy. These same attitudes spill over to the minister's wife and family as well.

Carried to extremes, the minister's symbolic role can come across in some pretty strange forms. At one end of the extreme, the minister may seem a godlike figure with almost superhuman powers. At the other end of the extreme, however, the minister rates as little more than a "holy go-between," carrying out religious rites when nothing else will do. Either extreme view makes people feel uncomfortable around ministers. You may have picked up on these kinds of feelings in social settings when persons in the group learn that you are a minister's wife. Have you ever noticed how the topic of conversation may shift when you come on the scene?

Part of the symbolic role idea has to do with fear of judgment. Some persons react as though being around a minister or his wife were the same thing as being in God's presence. People who feel this way may act ill at ease or try too hard to seem "religious" when with you or your husband. One pastor's wife exclaimed, "I wish people didn't feel they had to clean up their act on my account. I'm not their judge!" People may also lash out at the church by bringing up all the bad things they know about religion in general or clergy in particular. These reactions are often defense tactics to cover uneasy personal feelings. Even family members may react to you differently now that you are married to a minister.

Persons who look on clergy as holy go-betweens seem to have little respect for this vocation. They often think the minister doesn't work for a living and is really kind of useless. Their only contact with ministers usually comes at funerals, weddings, or public events where prayer is spoken. You may have met someone with this attitude and perhaps resented being talked down to or joked about in a not-so-funny way.

The symbolic role idea, whatever the degree of truth, tags your husband as the resident "holy man." Laypersons tend to resist accepting him as an ordinary mortal. An old joke lists three sexes: male, female, and clergy. It's not so funny to live with this exaggerated image day after day. In fact, people often relate more to their *idea* of the minister than to him or her as an individual.

## Heroic Role

People often want ministers to be rescuers or "fixers." When church programs lag or personal problems build to the point of crisis, many persons expect the minister to have the answer and make things right again. In this case the minister is far from useless—a virtual miracle worker, doing everything and doing it successfully. You may have heard this expectation from church members, perhaps in listening to them *before* you moved to the church field. One clergy couple being interviewed for church staff positions recalled hearing a shopping list of problems the congregation wanted them to solve right away.

Can it be wrong for congregations to look to their minister and his wife for the spark that may get their fellowship going? Isn't this what ministry is all about? Certainly a degree of high hope is to be expected. Carried to extremes, however, heroic hopes can push ministers and their wives to appear larger than life, like the cartoon characters on Saturday morning TV. In an age considered lacking in genuine heroes, such ideals may be tempting to pursue. But the process can be very stressful to live up to day after day. Real life usually doesn't have the easy solutions that TV good guys find. Ministers and their families can suffer burnout from trying to fill a superhuman role in all they do.

## Exemplary Role

Ministers serve as role models in living out biblical truths. They help make God's grace and purpose real in people's lives. One of the great opportunities for clergy couples is modeling an authentic Christian life-style. This aspect of ministry has been a central part of foreign missions work for years—showing by example how Christian faith works out in everyday events. The apostle Paul summed up a minister's life-style as "an example for the believers in your speech, your conduct, your love, faith, and purity" (1 Tim. 4:12).

Perhaps of all ideals of ministry, this exemplary role is easiest to carry to extremes because both clergy and laypersons seem eager to insist on it. Ministers can fall into the trap of becoming plaster saints. Behavior can quickly sink to the level of "appearance," based more on what people might think than on what is right. There is considerable pressure to act more like paragons of perfection than like sinners saved by grace. While serving as a perfect example sounds good and seems something ministers *ought* to do, it is unrealistic. Trying to be flawless in every word and deed is more burden than blessing. Christ didn't call His followers to sit on a pedestal but to let Him use their lives as working parts of His body on earth.

In addition to these popular ideas about ministers, congregations have some more basic standards for those serving as their leaders. These standards reach into the heart of the gospel's pattern for living. You will want to understand these expectations as they relate to your husband's serving and to your own role.

### General Role Expectations

Ministry does have ideals. Most Christians look to ministers for the highest and truest reflection of God's purpose. All Christians should act out of that same commitment, but those in ministry face higher standards because of their leadership role. Church members want to feel good about the persons who lead them. Such hope is reasonable and necessary in building trust. These ideals are fairly obvious but worth reviewing:

• *Good character.*—A minister's life-style needs to be consistent with Christian values. This does not mean sinless perfection, past or present, but rather a moral and ethical way of living. Church members look for this kind of character before they trust a minister with their confidence, hopes, and spiritual needs.

• *Active faith.*—Most church members would like to feel that their clergy are seeking God's direction. They trust that ministers are serving because of a deep sense of God's call and leadership. Signs of a minister's active faith help the congregation affirm his role as their spiritual leader and his work as God's servant.

• *Concern for others.*—Congregations usually want ministers who show positive, open, and caring attitudes. Effective ministry grows out of the ability to love and get along with all kinds of people.

• *Self-control.*—Ability to take an adult approach to situations is vital in a closely knit community such as a local church. Controlling personal behavior in a mature way goes along with building any kind of meaningful relationship but is especially needed in ministry settings. Coping with a variety of pressures, activities, and personalities calls for patience, understanding, tolerance, forgiveness, and kindness—all part of being "grown up" in the truest sense.

• *Willingness to serve.*—Ministers need to be self-starters with both skill and determination to follow through on their tasks. Ministry is not always bathed in the rosy glow of success. Many duties are routine and not particularly inspiring. Plans and projects sometimes drag on and on. People won't always respond in positive, supportive ways. A commitment to take on the role of minister, with all its ups and downs, is crucial to effective service.

These standards for ministers, plus popular notions about ministry, lay the background for your role as a clergy wife. Not much can be done about changing these widely held views, but much can be done in understanding and shaping your response to them. Your experience as a minister's wife may well have brought you into contact with some of these ideals. You might even be in conflict with some of them. Your skill in realizing the place of these expectations and in relating them to your role can be the key to your sense of satisfaction and fulfillment as a minister's wife.

At this point it might be a good idea to examine some of these ideals and standards as they relate directly to you as a minister's wife. General role expectations for you are usually shaped by the congregation's attitude toward ministry. But ministers' wives do have some freedom in finding their place in the church. You can learn to work with congregational expectations in a positive way.

• *Serving as a role model.*—Directly linked to the minister's exemplary role is the expectation that his wife will serve as an example for women and girls in the church. Even so, many church members will not expect more of you in this area than they do of any Christian woman. However, as the minister's wife you are likely to get more attention than other women in the congregation. You become a kind of celebrity in the community and therefore are more visible, more open to comparison with others. This is one of the givens of ministry you share. Wives of other public figures go through the same thing, though perhaps in different ways.

• *Personal faith.*—Church members generally look for some kind of religious commitment in their minister's wife. It supports their trust in the clergy couple for sound leadership, especially in denominations where the wife is expected to be an active part of the ministry team. You don't have to know every doctrine, interpret all the difficult Scripture passages, or even have a dramatic conversion experience to have an active faith. Many women become ministers' wives without long years of Christian service or a family background of regular church-going. At the time they married, about half of all ministers' wives did not know their husband would choose a religious vocation. At a retreat one pastor's wife told of her struggle during the early years of her husband's ministry because she was not a Christian at the time. Whatever your spiritual pilgrimage up to now, you can help meet the congregation's expectation by honestly defining your own faith. You can come to understand and respect the importance attached to this expectation by church members.

• *Showing concern.*—Most types of ministry call for high levels of involvement with people. Serving in a local church means building relationships. You don't have to like everyone as "best friends," but you will need to accept and get along with all kinds of people. If you feel less outgoing, don't lose heart. You can still find your special way to show love and care. Concern can be expressed in many different ways.

• *Willingness to serve.*—One of the best assets you can bring to your role is willingness to take on the job. No minister's wife can expect to find satisfaction or fulfillment if she has to be dragged kicking and screaming every inch of the way. Studies show that the number one family issue that compels ministers to leave their vocation is the wife's dissatisfaction with her role.

Some ministers' wives look on their role as God-called, as their way of serving. Others see themselves simply as persons who happen to be married to ministers. Still others seek a personal career in or out of the church. Women with any of these views can and do fill their role as a minister's wife quite successfully. Problems are likely to arise only if you perceive a clash between your minister's wife role and personal goals you may have set. At that point you might wish to examine your attitude toward ministry, commitment to your marriage, and willingness to balance these concerns in a sensible way. How would you approach these same issues if your husband had chosen to be an astronaut or a rodeo performer?

All ministers' wives have one thing in common—the need to relate in a meaningful way to their husband's chosen career. In some ways relating to a vocation in ministry means hard choices and adjustments. In other ways it is the most natural thing in the world to embrace your husband's call to ministry as you would any other important part of his life.

### Serving in a Local Church

A large majority of ministers' wives live in a local church setting. For that reason, a substantial portion of this text will focus on relationships at the congregational level. Most ministers at one time or another deal with local churches, in starting their career or in some leadership capacity. Getting some idea about the main concerns of congregations can be a good start on a positive response to your role.

Reading about ministry problems or listening to horror stories about unpleasant experiences in a few cases may give you the idea that serving in a local church is a big headache. While most ministry situations fall short of paradise, all have the potential of being good experiences. The secret seems to lie in coming to grips with expectations, your own and those of the church.

Congregational expectations at the local level largely revolve around the church's sense of direction and members' concept of how you should fit into that process. Two main points will be at the top of most congregations' checklist: attending worship services and supporting your husband's ministry. Each congregation will also have other ideas about your serving, but these two areas will be at the heart of them.

Ministers' wives are generally expected to be present for regular worship services. While this commitment applies to all church members, your presence is more apt to be noticed. Attendance at regular worship services is one of the more visible tokens used to measure any person's support for the church. Beyond the obvious expectation of your presence, however, lies the deeper idea that your attendance shows interest in the church and loyalty to your husband's ministry efforts.

Support for your husband's ministry is a second visible way congregations have of testing their expectations of you. Many church members tend to see the minister's wife in the traditional role of wife and mother. They may view your best way of helping your husband as that of home companionship and care. Even in denominations with a tradition of women ministers, the wife's loyalty to her husband's role remains unquestioned. Your identity as wife and mother is part and parcel of sharing ministry, regardless of how you may serve the church otherwise. You and your husband may not look on your role in these traditional terms, but you can count on the fact that many of the congregation do so.

Church members hope to see you undergirding your husband's efforts rather than pulling against him or competing with him. Many church members don't know how to relate to a minister's wife who comes on too strong in congregational activities. One layperson put it this way: "We called him to be our minister, not her."

Just how much activity on your part is too much or too little? The local situation determines this question to some degree, most often based on membership size and need for leadership. Most congregations, however, are willing to let the minister's wife set her own pace and decide her level of involvement. Laypersons from smaller churches sometimes expect more participation from their minister's wife—not an unusual hope where many tasks fall on a few persons. Congregants will appreciate your serving among them, but they won't expect you to do all the work or take on jobs no one else wants. Such activities as teaching, visiting, or serving in various organizations are looked on more as options than as essentials for most ministers' wives.

What about all those picky things you've heard about that church members expect—like entertaining, dressing a certain way, or giving devotionals at the drop of a hat? Some of that kind of expectation does exist; it "goes with the territory." But it is less of a problem than popular folklore would have you believe. Such expectations can be tactfully handled and are only as burdensome as you allow them to become.

Active, concerned church members generally feel that ministers' wives should have the same status in the church as any other member. Such openness shows a great deal of sensitivity on many members' part and also their willingness to let a minister's wife have elbow room in working out her place among them. However, taking advantage of this freedom does not come easy for many clergy wives. Feeling needed and being identified as "first lady" in the church can be strong motives to take on more and more responsibility—or lead to more and more guilt when less active. The power of leadership is addictive, and choosing to be "just one of the group" can be tough to accept.

Take comfort in the fact that most church members will support you in whatever role you choose for yourself. If you want to take a background role or be less active in the church, you can help the congregation understand and accept your decision. Congregations generally trust that their minister's wife will serve as God leads and equips her. This kind of trust should give you a great sense of freedom in seeking your most meaningful role.

## A Perspective on Expectations

The Bible doesn't go into detail about ministers' wives. The apostle Peter's wife and Priscilla are among the few named in the New Testament. The apostle Paul noted that wives went along with the apostles and the Lord's brothers when they traveled on church business (1 Cor. 9:5). Beyond this bit of information, little is known of these women's service.

The New Testament sets out a few expectations for wives of church leaders, though these ideals are described more in terms of character than of church responsibility. Such traits as personal purity and integrity (1 Tim. 3:11), holy living and self-control (Titus 2:3,5), and inner beauty (1 Pet. 3:4) are typical concepts. An overall air of wholesomeness, decency, and purpose seemed to surround the service of Bible wives, mothers, and church women.

These New Testament principles, however, tell us little about the women as individuals—how they lived, what they felt, or how they went about sharing ministry with their husbands. Christian freedom, gifting by the Holy Spirit, and spiritual wisdom surely enabled New Testament women to transcend social pressures and limitations of their day. Their lives surely left an impact on the church and created a legacy for us today. A roll call of Christian women down through the centuries can remind us of their courage and faith.

Sharing ministry is a noble undertaking. Like all spiritual riches, this gift is held in a common clay pot, as the apostle Paul so wisely observed. Serving as a symbol, a hero, or an example can get out of hand if we do not realize the truth of Paul's words. Often church members fear too much humanness in their clergy couple, and many clergy couples often fear the challenge of being truly human as Christ lived. Yet this is how ministers and their mates serve best—by reaching out to others through who they are as persons, as unique individuals with every weakness and strength common to humanity. Who you are is not a barrier to being a minister's wife unless you choose to make it so.

Biblical concepts of ministry are based on

servanthood—of being God's instrument of grace and reconciliation in a broken world. Such a role requires an ongoing quest for spiritual truth and maturity. This kind of biblical expectation doesn't put a lot of artificial standards on you or twist your identity all out of shape. Rather, biblical expectations look on your personhood as a gift to be used in the community of faith: "There are different ways of serving, but the same Lord is served. There are different abilities to perform service, but the same God gives ability to everyone for their particular service. The Spirit's presence is shown in some way in each person for the good of all" (1 Cor. 12:5-7).

All expectations of ministers' wives, yours or the church's, need to be brought under this truth of God's grace. Whatever role you are called to fill as minister's wife can be personally and communally fulfilling when based on God's leading.

## **Time Out**

What were your feelings when you first learned you would be a minister's wife?

How do those feelings relate to your present idea of what a minister's wife should be and do?

*Take time to review your feelings and expectations as a minister's wife. Then place these concerns under God's grace:*

Dear Father, You have led me to this place of serving. Now give me the wisdom, strength, and love to share ministry with my husband and with Jesus Christ.

# 2

# Starting Out, Settling In

*Joan picked at her food. She had a queasy feeling inside. Her pregnancy was partly to blame, but facing these strangers on the church personnel committee was the main reason. They represented Todd's first opportunity for a full-time church position with an adequate staff and facilities. She desperately wanted to avoid saying or doing anything to lessen his chance for the job. Yet everything she said seemed either overly eager or stupid. "Who are these people, and what do they expect of me?" Joan wondered. "Even if we move to this church, will I ever fit in? I'm doomed! I'm just not the typical minister's wife."*

Being a minister's wife is more than being married to someone in a church vocation. It also means sharing a special kind of relationship with people. These people may be in a church congregation, a mission field, a denominational agency, or some other group with whom your husband carries out his ministry. Your challenge lies in making that relationship a good one.

Your attitude toward your role sets the tone for the way you respond to the people under your husband's charge. You may see your role as a minister's wife implying nothing more than casual involvement in your husband's ministry. You will still need to get off to a good start in every place your husband serves. If you see your role as a mission—your way of serving—then you will want especially to make the most of relationships.

Some practical steps can be taken to ease the strain of moving into a new setting. You can make the most of opportunities to build loving, supportive relationships. These steps apply if you are in a student pastorate, first ministry field, or changing service locale at any point along the way.

## Meeting and Greeting

Don't let anyone fool you: Coming into new settings is awkward on everyone involved. So much newness has to be faced, so many changes to cope with all at once. How do you survive the move with minimum upset? Simply by getting organized for the move as far in advance as possible. Planning is the key to a smooth transition from one place to another. Along with the physical moving of self and belongings goes an emotional move. This inner sense of place and identity needs to be handled as carefully as your most prized household item.

One of the best ways of meeting new people and places is to say a healthy good-bye to old surroundings. Saying good-bye won't mean cutting off the past forever, but it will mean letting go in a gracious way. Leaving either a good or a bad situation can be distressing. Problems often follow when the old setting intrudes into the new. Let's look at some ways to make a good move.

## Getting Ready to Go

Before you face a move, even before one is a remote possibility, think about the idea. Acting as though things will stay the same forever can be a costly error. Ministry is not one of the more predictable careers! Thinking about moving helps you deal with the idea. It's kind of like looking up the answer in the back of the book—you know what to expect.

Preparing children for a move is very important. Talk to them early on about the kind of career their father has chosen. Explain that moving to different places is part of that work. Ask your children to express their feelings about the idea of moving. Help them think of ways to deal with feelings of anger, anxiety, or sadness. Suggest some positive benefits of going to new places and meeting new friends. Discuss ways of keeping in touch with family or friends who would be left behind.

Small children have fears about leaving everything behind or being left themselves. Talk about what might happen with pets, favorite belongings, hobbies, special places to eat, school, visits with grandparents, and other everyday happenings in your family's life when you move. Explain that some changes will be necessary but that many favorite possessions and activities can still be enjoyed in the new home. Putting a positive outlook on moving helps children deal with it in a less traumatic way. Check the library or book store for some children's books about moving. Read and discuss them with your children. Lots of valuable insights can be found to make moving more enjoyable.

Look ahead to the next likely step in your husband's career: graduation from school or seminary, first ministry assignment, first full-time position, change of church or vocation, and so on. What will this career step mean in terms of family, social, and vocational life? What likely changes will it bring about? What will help get ready for this change?

Thinking about the possibility of a move focuses on the wider issues involved. You can deal with the most dreaded parts of moving before they happen. Then when the move actually comes along, you'll have a lot of the anxiety under control. You can find effective ways of coping with this break in your life. This way of looking at moves may seem overly simple, but the process can take a lot of the grief out of leaving.

### Before the Van Arrives

Moving is hectic at best, disastrous at worst. The more you can do ahead of moving day to get ready, the better off you'll be. Begin by finding out who will handle, finance, and direct the move. Some churches and agencies

make all the arrangements, including the choice of mover. You may have to make these arrangements or do the moving yourself. But have it clearly understood who does what and, especially, who pays for what. Professional movers expect to be paid at unloading time. The shock can be rough indeed if you're handed the bill with no means to cover it.

If you are in charge of the move, shop around before choosing either a professional mover or renting needed equipment. Ask friends about their experience with local companies. Estimate what equipment will be needed to handle your goods if moving yourself. Allow a little extra to be on the safe side. Most families have more stuff than they usually think they do. Ask professional movers for any helps they offer. Some companies provide booklets on packing tips, box labels, lists of necessary steps to take, and other time-savers as part of their service.

Packing your own possessions can bring peace of mind as well as cut expenses. Even if using professional movers, you might want to carry family heirlooms and special items yourself. Pack less used items first. This is also a good time to set aside items for a yard sale or charity donation. Let your children pack and mark some of their favorite things for easy locating in the new home. Clearly label boxes or use colored tape to identify ones to be opened first. The main rules of doing your own packing: Allow plenty of time, don't overcrowd boxes, and use plenty of paper to cushion items. Your loving care often makes for better packing.

Plan the last three days in your old home and the first three in the new one. Set out needed clothing; medicines and personal care items; needed financial, school, or medical records; and a few favorite games and toys for the children. Plan some quick, simple meals. Make sleeping arrangements if unable to stay in the home. Try to keep these days free of business or ministry responsibilities. Allow extra time for last-minute snags and, especially, for rest.

Accept help from friends in running errands, child care, or providing meals. Helping you is one way friends can adjust to your leaving and work through their feelings. Take pictures or revisit favorite places to celebrate the good times in the place you leave. These memories provide a needed tie with the past and help encourage new pleasures to come.

### Making a Good Entrance

Moving creates some special issues for ministers' wives. As you enter a new ministry area, think about what your coming says to persons there. Their familiar routine of relating is changing just as much as yours. They still hold feelings about the former minister and his wife. You will be living in her shadow for some time to come. Take time to let feelings sort out. Be patient with both the new people and yourself in getting to know one another.

Consider the kind of experience the people had with the former minister and his family. Accept the situation, whether good or bad, and give people the chance to make a new beginning with you. Let the church love and appreciate the former minister's wife. These good feelings need not be a barrier to your own place among them. Rejoice with the church's concern for this fellow helpmeet. Don't force the people to choose between you and this well-remembered minister's wife.

Realize that if experiences with the former minister and his wife were not good, the people may need quite some time for feelings to heal. You may not win their trust and acceptance right away. If feelings toward you are distant or hesitant at first, you are probably not the cause. Leftover emotions may still be strong among the people. Allow these feelings to settle before claiming your special place.

A minister's leaving usually triggers a sharp break in the life of a congregation. The church generally goes through a grief process, even if the parting were less than happy. Don't expect to immediately take the place of the former minister's wife in the life of the church. Take it in good grace when you are compared with her: "You were so fortunate to have had someone with her talents. My gifts lie along other lines." Or, "Recent experiences seem to be of great concern to you. I hope you will allow me

time to learn how I can best serve with you."

Also realize that you may be dealing with strong feelings of your own: leaving home, seminary, employment, friends, and the like. You are going through your own grief process in leaving a familiar situation. Give yourself time to adjust and clear up mixed feelings. Affirm the things you enjoyed and will miss: people, favorite places, good times, and special events. Let these experiences provide some good clues on building new relationships. For example: "I was so tied up in my job, I really didn't take advantage of all the good things our old hometown had to offer. I need to be more appreciative here." Or: "Pat turned out to be my best friend. At first I thought she had a weird way of doing things, and I almost missed out on a great relationship. Maybe I ought to take a more sensitive look at new friends here."

If you left an unpleasant situation, don't hold it against this new place. Resist taking out anger, resentment, and hurt feelings on new acquaintances. Don't automatically expect these people to be like the old group. If you're getting over a deep hurt, don't rush into new relationships. This haste can be as unwise as rejecting people. Allow your feelings to fall into perspective. One minister's wife confessed that she needed two years to think calmly about a church group who fired her husband. Many wives share similar feelings about unhappy ministry experiences that left them gun-shy about new relationships.

Take special care if you did not want to leave the former place of ministry. Your resistance to the new setting may have unfortunate consequences on your family's adjustment, as well as on your husband's ministry. Give the situation a chance to pan out. You won't want to shut off the possibility of great blessings God may be leading you to claim.

### Settling In

The first months of a new ministry are sometimes called the "honeymoon," or start-up stage. During this time first contacts are made with the new group of people. These early contacts provide a chance for getting to know each other, testing feelings, and laying the ground-work for a continuing relationship. These early experiences are important in defining your role.

If at all possible, keep these earliest days free of church responsibilities. Give yourself time to settle into your new home. You may need to spend more time with your children than expected, for example. If you work outside the home, this new job may need its own adjustment phase. You will want some flexibility in coping with these demands. You will also benefit from less pressure to perform so soon after moving.

Learning about the new ministry situation is important before plunging into a full load of church tasks. Allow time to get a feel for relationships, mood of the group, and how you can best fit into that setting. One new educational minister's wife, herself a trained youth minister, was asked to take over leadership of a youth Sunday School group immediately on her arrival. Hard feelings among leaders in that department resulted in the former leader's resignation. Though fully capable of doing the task, the minister's wife declined to step in.

Stepping in so quickly could have created an even more tense situation. Acting without knowing the people involved might have made later relationships difficult, at best. When the youth leaders saw that the new minister and his wife weren't going to take sides, they worked out their problem among themselves. Later the minister's wife did work with the youth group, but only after her presence presented no threat to other leaders.

Older church members usually take delight in telling the congregation's history. Take advantage of the opportunity to find out about the church's roots, founding families, and times of victory or grief. Every church group has a power structure of influential individuals. These persons may or may not hold official positions in the congregation. Get some idea of who sets the trends and gives direction to group decisions. Churches also have traditions and "sacred cows" that affect relationships. Learning about these can be insightful

and keep you from blundering into an awkward situation.

**Letting People Know Who You Are**

Early days in a ministry setting are equally important in letting people find out about you. These days give the best chance to state your role preferences, to indicate the part you wish to play in your husband's ministry. If you are new to the congregation, you can start off in any way you choose. For example, you can change your level of activity from that of a former ministry setting: "I took on too many jobs in our last church. I'm going to take on one job and enjoy it."

You can let people know what you wish to be called. Some ministers and their wives prefer a formal name: "Pastor and Mrs. Brown." Others want first-name informality: "Ted and Mary Jane." Remember, though, that some people will stick to their choice rather than yours. Many people prefer formal address out of respect for the office of minister. If that is their reasoning, appreciate and accept the honor even if you'd prefer use of your given name.

If you wish casual callers in your home, let people know you'd like them to drop in. Indicate your wants or needs for companionship. For example, "I like to jog before breakfast. Is there anyone in the neighborhood willing to join me?" Or, "I really enjoy a cup of tea about 9:30 in the morning. Who's free to drop by?"

Keeping some nights free for family activities can just as easily be made clear. You may be asked your preference but if not, you can explain: "Friday nights are our family time. We support our kids in their sports program and eat pizza afterward. We think this time together is very important for us, and we don't usually make other appointments." Or: "John and I eat lunch out every Thursday. It's our time as a couple to keep in touch with each other." When church members know you have a special family time, they are less likely to intrude on it. Some ministers print a schedule in the church newsletter.

Early days on the ministry field can be days

of grace. Use them to take stock of your needs in your new surroundings. Take plenty of time before committing to a work load. Settling in can be much smoother when family members move at their own pace. Entering new church life, school, social groups, and home tasks means making a lot of adjustment. Take advantage of your freedom as a newcomer to move in gracefully and comfortably.

### Building a Support System

One of the things making a move so traumatic is the loss of support from a familiar, caring group. Family, neighbors, and congregational friends get left behind. Community professional helpers such as doctors, dentists, lawyers, bankers, or hairdressers take on a comfortable identity after longtime association. Replacing them in a new place can be a real hassle. You may feel uneasy until these bases of support are back in place. You will want to get a new support system going as soon as possible. Doing so brings encouragement, a sense of security, and a better introduction into the new community.

Look for persons in the new setting who can help you get acquainted and feel "at home." You will feel more secure when you've located a few trusted people you can call for help. Some quick possibilities are fellow staff ministers and their wives. They had to go through the same adjustment to moving and likely know the shortcuts to settling in. Other support persons might be found among members of the call committee or church board who brought your husband to his new position. Their support is likely since they recommended you to the church. Other supporters may come from your Sunday School class or church women's groups. Church officers, deacons, elders, or the like should be willing to help by providing information or assistance.

Respond to people who offer practical help. Ask someone to help you locate good shopping areas, your children's school, medical facilities, and the like. One pastor's wife came to appreciate an elderly lady's list of "most reliable" helpers such as an appliance repairman,

plumber, electrician, and auto mechanic. One former minister's wife left a "who to call if" list taped to the kitchen cabinet in the church parsonage. One of the listed items: "If you need a good laugh or cry."

Social as well as practical help might be available from other ministers' wives in the area. Make contact with the ministers' wives group for your denomination if one is available. Your husband will likely have contact with a ministers' group. See what contact the wives have through this group.

Other early social support might come from community persons who share common concerns. Check out church or neighboring families with children the same age as your own. If you belong to a national organization, get in touch with a local group. These and similar contacts can give an added sense of belonging in your new residence.

### Learning and Handling Role Demands

Most congregations fail to put into words what they expect of a minister's wife. They often go by past experience in deciding what they like or don't like for her to do. So finding out what a church expects of you is not always simple. However, you can discover their expectations and also help them understand your own ideas about serving as their minister's wife.

The best time to learn a church's expectations is during your husband's first dealings with the search committee or board. Your husband will negotiate his own role at this time, and he can state your role preferences as part of his ministry. These first contacts with church members are crucial in making your needs clearly known. Being direct, open, and honest in early discussions allows both you and the church to understand each other's wants and needs.

If you get to meet members of the search committee or other church leadership, ask what will be expected of you. Often you may get a vague, noncommittal answer: "Oh, nothing in particular. Just be a good helper to your husband." You can clear up such answers by moving talk in more specific ways. Ask what former ministers' wives did in the church. Ask if their level of activity were satisfactory, and why or why not. If you visit the church field, ask any staff members about the church's demands on their wives and families. Listen to what church members say about their hopes in your coming. Example: "Our last minister's wife played the organ so beautifully, and we're hoping you'll lead our music program, too." That's an ideal opening for you to state your intended role. Respond to such openings candidly. Word of your reply will get around. Forthright statements on your part will keep church members from being either disappointed or overly expectant.

Wives sometimes do not get to meet church leaders or visit the church prior to their husband's call. In that case, have your husband inquire about your role. Some ministers now request that the wife's role be written into the church's formal call to him. Let your husband express your shared ideas on ways you intend to support his ministry or relate to the church. The point is to avoid creating the wrong impression about what you can or will do. It is unwise to suggest a certain level of achievement and then be stuck trying to live up to it. Let limitations on your serving be understood: personal choice, health problems, child care, career, educational goals, and the like. Much less upset comes from learning congregation reaction to your wishes *before* coming to the church than afterward. You can then assess the difficulties that your role choices might cause in the church.

If you expect to have a career of your own, this needs to be stated from the start. Some congregations view the minister's wife in traditional roles of wife and mother at home. Your decision about a career need not be a barrier to such congregations, but they need to assess their feelings from the start. They may expect you to attend day meetings for church women's groups, for example. Or, your employment might call for absence on Sundays or other regular worship times.

Taking an out-of-the-ordinary part in your husband's ministry might also call for early explanation. For example, one pastor and his wife shared worship leadership duties. She served as organist, planned the worship services, and directed choral selections. This working arrangement was not made clear during his negotiation with the church prior to accepting the position. On arrival at the church he was faced with doing without his wife's services or upsetting the music personnel already serving.

If serious conflict exists between your wishes and those of the church, you will want to weigh the consequences. Should your husband take the position, would the church's expectations be unacceptable to either or both of you? Would your sense of God's leading be denied by going along with the church's wishes? Are you willing to abide by the church's view of your role? Can you accept such demands as part of your shared life in ministry with your husband? Could you work out your role within that framework, even if it means putting aside some of your preferences?

Before cutting off the possibility of getting along with a congregation, make sure you have stated genuine role needs and not just personal whims. Be sure you've heard the church's view with sensitivity and understanding. Usually when both sides make realistic needs known, a mutual agreement can be worked out. Most congregations want their minister and his family to be happy in serving, but they also need that same feeling for themselves.

Unless you're a salaried employee of the church with a set job description, you should be able to decide what role you'll take and how active you'll be. If, however, you and your husband sense a serious and continuing disharmony with the church, you might give some thought to declining the position. One minister and his wife failed to pick up on signs from the congregation about their chosen life-style. They assumed people would get used to their unconventional marriage and career arrangements. This assumption soon proved very painful for both the couple and congregation. An early attempt at understanding role expectations can prevent such unfortunate events.

By all means yield your expectations to the Holy Spirit in considering your role. God is not likely to thrust you into a situation that threatens either your marriage or personal integrity. But you can create unnecessary problems for yourself by clinging to selfish or unrealistic ideas.

Role needs can change after moving to a church. You need not be locked into a set pattern forever. Talk about role needs with your husband. Work out the most mutually satisfactory level of involvement. Let him go to bat for you with church leaders. Ask trusted, spiritually wise church friends what they think about your role and what church members may be saying. You might be relieved to discover less demand from church members than you thought.

Coming to serve in a church can seem like an awesome task. But you can make an enjoyable place for yourself anywhere with tact and forethought. You can let the congregation know who you are and what you hope to do in sharing ministry with your husband. You can make needs known. You can serve in your own right. You can feel good about your chosen role when God's grace and purpose lie behind your choice: "But have reverence for Christ in your hearts, and honor him as Lord. Be ready at all times to answer anyone who asks you to explain the hope you have in you, but do it with gentleness and respect" (1 Pet. 3:15-16).

Finally, comfort yourself with the fact that you can't possibly meet every church member's expectation. Some part of your life-style, behavior, personality, appearance, and way of serving will attract unfavorable comments from a few individuals. A retired minister's wife lightheartedly noted: "About five percent of the people love absolutely everything you do. Another five percent can't stand you. And the rest probably don't give a hoot. So be yourself, and let God take care of the rest."

### Time Out

What part of being a minister's wife bothers you most?

When you go to a new ministry setting, what can you do to ease this bothersome barrier?

Who can you ask to help you be yourself?

*Take time to think about your role as a minister's wife. Focus on your greatest anxieties. Then weigh them in the scales with God's grace:*

Dear Father, God of wisdom and of love, shine Your light on my role. Thank You for sharing my struggles through Your Holy Spirit and for showing signs of Your care through those who offer me their support.

# 3

# Presenting a Positive Self-Image

*Joan slumped on the couch. She was caught between frustration and tears. This had been one of those days when nothing seemed to go right. Her presentation at the church women's meeting never got off the ground. At the potluck luncheon afterward her raw vegetable dish was called "rabbit food." Table talk seemed to center on what a marvelous, talented, friendly, and saintly woman the former minister's wife had been. To top it all off, dinner that evening turned out a disaster. Their hostess had said on the phone, "We'll be eating on the patio," so Joan dressed casually. Everyone else showed up dressed to the teeth, and it was no picnic! "What's wrong with me?" Joan wondered. "I feel so useless and stupid. Why can't I just be myself? I'm not sure I can make it as a minister's wife."*

We all want to feel accepted as a person in our own right, to feel good about ourselves in comparison to others. We want to project a positive self-image that others respond to with respect if not appreciation. These desires are some of the first steps toward personhood any human being takes. The process begins in infancy and lasts a lifetime.

Your awareness of self can get lost in the many private and public roles you play: minister's wife, church worker, mate, mother, friend, employee, club member, daughter, sister, and so on. You may have to put on a different outer image in filling these separate and varying roles. You may have to look, talk, relate, and react differently in each area. You may soon find yourself wishing, "Will the real *me* please stand up!"

The goal of this chapter is to help you take a good look at yourself and affirm the unique person you are. Defining identity and self-esteem are the focus of this process. Give yourself permission to journey inward, to know and love yourself.

## Affirming Selfhood

You are a unique, separate self from all others. To say this is easy, but to realize this fact's impact on everyday life is not so simple. Yet finding your identity is essential in knowing who you are and who you can become. You need to affirm in yourself:

- who I am
- my worth as a person among others
- my strengths and gifts
- my weaknesses
- my potential
- my inner direction and spiritual purpose

Failure to affirm these vital points results in a limited or distorted sense of self. You may appear to yourself like the figure in a fun house mirror, all grotesque or unlovely. Or, you may pump up your ego to giant size and overrate your importance. Both these extremes grow out of failure to know and accept yourself as a person. Unless you can feel at ease in your own identity, you may try to copy someone else's personality. Then you may feel shallow as a person like those the apostle Paul described who were "carried by the waves and blown about by every shifting wind" (Eph. 4:14).

Learning about yourself helps you to:

*1. Establish individuality.*—You have a unique set of physical, mental, and spiritual factors. These traits are the building blocks of selfhood. They affect how you came to be who you are. Understanding yourself means owning these factors which make you an individual.

*2. Build relationships.*—How you see yourself influences how you see others. If you don't think much of yourself, you likely won't think much of those around you. Relating well to others begins with knowing your own worth and grows as you acknowledge the physical, mental, and spiritual factors which make others who they are as persons.

*3. Make decisions and set priorities.*—Knowing who you are helps decide where you want to go with your life. Then you can pinpoint those things in life that are important to you. Energy and resources can be used in ways that undergird your needs and goals.

*4. Give life direction.*—Making choices and setting goals should fairly reflect who you are, to be sure, but also who you have the potential to become by God's grace. You probably have some idea of what you can and cannot do, but you also need to allow room to test the limits of your abilities and gifts. Your life will take an ultimate direction whether you drift or set your sights. How much more fulfilling to let spiritual wisdom affirm the person you are and give your life purpose.

Your identity is made up of all those elements that make you unique (physical, mental, social, spiritual). Some of those factors may not be exactly as you'd like. But all parts of your identity are valuable in self-understanding, whether you think they are negative or positive. The apostle Paul noted, "But by God's grace I am what I am, and the grace that he gave me was not without effect" (1 Cor. 15:10). You have the challenge of claiming your identity and growing within its potential as God leads.

Let's look at some ways you can go about affirming your identity. A good starting place is discovering the persons and events that influenced you when you were very young.

**Reclaiming Your Roots**

You received a set of genetic givens from your biological parents—nervous system, physical appearance, intellectual capacities, general health pattern, and other inborn traits. These parts of your identity are more or less fixed. Beyond these genetic factors, you also received social and psychological cues from those who cared for you as a small child. You used these cues to form your behavior, outlook on the world around you, and ideas about yourself as a person. This early self-image plays an important part in your present sense of worth and identity.

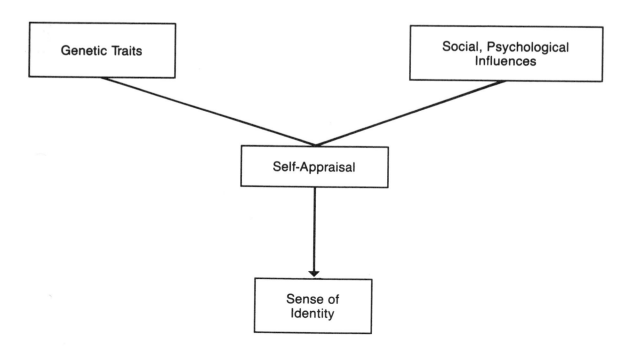

Your past added its flavor to your personality makeup. Part of Christian maturity lies in finding redemptive meaning in past experiences. Painful or unpleasant areas of the past are often hard to face comfortably. Feelings of anger, guilt, shame, or anxiety may cling to these tender spots. Yet accepting and understanding these areas can free you to be more of yourself now. Ask yourself the following questions and answer them as fully and accurately as you can:

- What kind of person was I as a child?
- How did my parents/family respond to me?
- What persons did I choose as role models?
- What kind of person did my friends and adults indicate I was?

These questions focus on impressions of self gained from persons who played an important part in your early years. Responses from them helped shape your feelings of self-worth. Positive responses probably gave you confidence in yourself. Negative responses may have undercut your confidence and made you uncertain about yourself. Whatever responses you received as a child still play a part in your present self-image.

Describe yourself as a child. Were you pleased with yourself in comparison with others your age? If not, why? What about your appearance, skills, and behavior at that time? Did you often feel good about yourself as a person? Do you still feel much the same way about yourself?

Think about your place in the scheme of things at home as a child. Were you loved, nurtured, respected as an individual, and accepted for who you were? Were you able to please your parents, teachers, or other important adults? Were you favorably or unfavorably compared with other children by these key adults? Were you allowed to make some choices, encouraged to take responsibility for your actions, and helped to work through errors in a constructive way? Were you listened to or able to express feelings? Did you feel that you were understood and treated fairly? Were your achievements noted or praised in the family group?

Recall the role models you used to measure yourself. Were these role models realistic examples to copy—that is, someone you had a fair chance to measure up to? Did comparing yourself with these models make you feel good or bad about yourself? What did these models cause you to choose as goals for your life? From whom did you take your behavior cues?

Finally, describe the type of person you think others saw you to be as a child. Did friends and schoolmates shun you or want to include you in their activities? How well did you fit into the group? Did you feel accepted by the community in which you lived? Did you feel at ease in social settings?

Negative impressions of self gained in childhood often endure as emotional burdens carried into adult years. As a result, present responses are often made in light of past experiences. Place any negative impressions you may hold of yourself in perspective. Are these ideas accurate? Are they true at this stage in your life or have you outgrown them? Is someone—parent, family member, friend—still making you feel like an awkward little kid? If so, see if present facts about yourself support such an idea. Get rid of any false impressions about yourself carried over from childhood, or take time to reinterpret impressions in light of the present. If the ugly duckling has turned into a swan, stop thinking of yourself as a duck.

One of the most touching accounts in the Old Testament tells of Esau's desire for his father's blessing. Esau's brother Jacob got hold of the patriarchal blessing through trickery. Esau begged Isaac, "Bless me too, father!" (Gen. 27:38). Loss of his father's blessing left Esau with a sense of despair and anger. Psychologically speaking, many adults face this same problem, growing up without a sense of approval ("blessing") from one or both parents. Nothing they did as a child seemed to please or satisfy their parents' expectation. As a result, they live under a cloud of anger and distress.

If you sense a lack of parental blessing, you may still be trying to achieve it—even if the critical parent is no longer living. You may be choosing your present life-style, planning your activities, or measuring your success by that parent's standards. This continual striving for parental approval can create stress, self-defeat, and lack of fulfillment. Or, you may be reacting to older persons (especially those you view as authority figures) in the same way as that critical parent.

You can take some steps to settle inner struggles about parental blessing. First, you might face the issue with your parent and try to achieve an agreeable balance between you. If confronting the parent seems too painful or possibly unworkable, express your feelings to a trusted older friend. Let that person affirm you in your parent's stead. A simple process can be useful if the critical parent is now deceased. Pretend that the critical parent is seated across from you as you verbally express feelings. The point is to acknowledge your feelings and clear the air between you and your parent. Owning your feelings openly can allow you to "leave home" emotionally and to affirm your present role as an adult. You can then feel freer in relating to parents or other authority figures.

Reclaim your roots by counting the wisdom and insight to be gained from past experiences. Free yourself from guilt over past missteps. Unresolved guilt feelings can be surrendered to God's mercy and love. Nothing you may have done is beyond Christ's atoning power. The New Testament lists a variety of sins committed by some persons before they became part of the Christian fellowship: murder, greed, theft, sexual perversion, adultery, drunkenness, idolatry. But along with the list of sinful acts came a message of grace: "You have been purified from sin; you have been dedicated to God; you have been put right with God by the Lord Jesus Christ and by the Spirit of our God" (1 Cor. 6:11). You can accept this healing and cleansing in your life as God's grace gift.

Placing your past in God's care allows you to look back on it with understanding and peace. The humorist Grady Nutt suggested not knocking the forerunner. He meant that what went before in your life brought you where you are today. This is something worth accepting and building on.

### Accepting Affirmation

One way of putting yourself down is by rejecting praise or affirmation from others. As a minister's wife, you likely get a lot of glib flattery. Yet even this kind of affirmation needs to be accepted at face value and enjoyed. Others see a side of you which you do not or perhaps cannot know. Let them share their insights about you. Open yourself to their interest and pleasure in you as a person.

Find some trusted friends with whom you can be yourself. Share your concerns with them. Listen to their reflections about you. Enjoy their support and encouragement, but also hear their criticisms and suggestions. You may dread hearing criticism, but your gain in self-awareness is worth the risk of occasional disappointment or pain. If persons care enough to confront you in a loving way, rejoice in finding true friends; they have your best interests at heart.

Respond graciously to praise and approval. Some people reject compliments out of a false sense of modesty. But compliments help affirm your worth. Express your appreciation: "You made my day." Or: "I'm glad you feel that way. It makes me feel good to know!" When you have done well, say so within yourself and let others praise your achievements.

### Acknowledging Worth

Accept your worth as an individual. Little will be gained by either putting yourself down or exaggerating your abilities. But much can be gained by seeing yourself in a realistic way. After all, no one is without flaws. Some persons happen to be better organized, adjusted, or focused than others, yet even they don't bat a thousand all the time! Everyone faces crises in aging, learning, changing, and adapting to life's demands. You have just as much need to claim your proper place as anyone else.

Take some time to do a personal inventory. List your personal assets. Also list weaknesses or liabilities. Weigh them carefully, letting God's grace balance the scales!

| Assets | Liabilities |
|---|---|
| | |

Assets + Liabilities + God's grace = Potential

Think about the insight to be found in both assets and liabilities. Both tell you something about yourself, form part of your uniqueness, and measure your capacity to do certain things. Have you overlooked talents, skills, or gifts? These assets may have been denied out of false modesty or anxiety about using them. Have you put too much emphasis on your liabilities? Are you comparing yourself unfairly to others? Do you use an unnecessarily high standard because of your role as a minister's wife? Have you underestimated your potential by focusing most of your attention on what you cannot do rather than on what you can do?

A careful look at the lives of biblical leaders will show all kinds of flaws, faults, and failings. But God did not see these liabilities as a barrier to serving. God did ask for trust, commitment, and obedience so that His enabling could take hold in their lives. The same option is open to you.

### Gaining Self-Esteem

You are probably keenly aware of your need for food, water, air, clothing, shelter, and other basics for survival. You may be less aware, however, of basic psychological needs. Inner needs don't always make such insistent de-

mands on you as do hunger or thirst. Yet failing to meet psychological needs can create inward pain and loss.

A primary psychological need is to think well of yourself. This need can be met at a surface level through approval by others. To really feel good about yourself at a deep level, however, you need a sense of achievement and purpose in life. When you have that sense of worth, you have self-esteem. You can feel competent and valuable as a person.

### Understanding Self-Esteem

Psychologists identify some basic ways of gaining a sense of self-worth. These ways center around making achievements, taking some control over events in your life, having good relationships, and acting on your deepest-held beliefs. Check out these areas in your self-image:

*1. Making achievements.*—Feeling good about yourself comes easily when your efforts turn out well. Seeing accomplishments result from personal actions gives you a sense of strength in coping with daily responsibilities. You gain confidence in your ability to tackle future tasks. Lack of achievement can produce the opposite feeling—that you cannot cope, have little or no choice, and probably won't do very well at most tasks.

Achievements are important to your sense of self-worth because they are perhaps the most visible and quickest tests of how you measure up to others. Earning self-esteem through accomplishments is valid, but it has limitations. What happens when you don't perform well? Suppose an accident or illness robs you of the capacity to act. How would you feel about yourself in such situations?

2. *Being in control.*—This part of self-esteem is often harder to affirm than achievements because it involves forces outside yourself. Being in control means that you have some influence on persons and events in your life. Esteem comes when your presence, personality, suggestions, or actions are welcomed by others. Respect from others indicates that you have good standing in the group. These positive forces give you a sense of choice or option about what you do. You feel that you are part of the decision-making process. A lack in this area can produce feelings of powerlessness, isolation, or helplessness.

3. *Having good relationships.*—Relationships carry the idea of esteem a step further to include the way others respond to you as a person. Esteem comes when you feel accepted, loved, wanted, and valued by those around you. Your sense of worth grows as others show interest, approval, and affection toward you. Such response gives a feeling of security in relating, even during times of crisis or personal failure. Further, your inner sense of worth is affirmed: "I think I'm OK, and others do too." Lack of meaningful relationships or difficulty in forming them can result in feelings of insecurity, rejection, or hopelessness.

4. *Acting on beliefs.*—Part of self-esteem comes from expressing your beliefs and religious convictions. A sense of satisfaction and fulfillment comes when you can define your beliefs, live by your principles, and make value judgments. Added esteem comes when others acknowledge and respect your beliefs. Lack of esteem in this area often shows up as lack of conviction about the important issues of life. Persons without a strong sense of personal

worth often manipulate others, avoid taking a stand, and go along with the crowd in decision making.

These four broad areas of self-esteem show the practical value of feeling good about yourself. Feeling worthy as a person is not the same as self-centeredness. Self-esteem affirms the person you are, while self-centeredness asserts personal wants or importance over others. In fact, self-esteem can be the best tool in fighting self-centeredness. When you know who you are and feel good about it, you won't need to lord it over others. You can relate without needing to dominate.

In short, self-esteem is the kind of reputation you have with yourself. You decide this reputation by adding up self-concepts, responses from other, experiences, and ideals. To the extent that you can feel good about yourself, you have positive self-esteem. Feelings of failure, rejection, or worthlessness indicate negative self-esteem. At one time or another all of us fail to succeed, get our point across, fit in, or follow our better judgment. These lapses are normal and not a sign of worthlessness. Continuing negative feelings about self, however, show a poor self-image. A new, redemptive look at self would be called for. Self-esteem needs to rest on a fairly consistent base of positive response in all areas of life. That doesn't mean that every day will be sunny. Rather, a sense of inner worth can lift you up and carry you through the stormy times that come along.

Building positive self-esteem is a goal in affirming your selfhood. Meeting this deep inner need frees you to grow as a person, work toward your potential, and reach out to others with genuine concern. Let's turn to some ways of bringing about this positive side of esteem.

### Building Self-Esteem

Gaining a sense of worth begins by taking a realistic look at yourself. Realistic doesn't mean ruthless or haphazard digging for faults. Realistic means accurate and fair assessment of your abilities, as well as looking for shortcomings.

Your role as a minister's wife can be ideal for

building self-esteem—through your own efforts and through the affirmation of others. Look for ways that you might use to enhance your feelings of worth.

• *Achievements.*—Review the opportunities you have for making accomplishments. Check these areas: home, church, social groups, hobbies, continuing education, civic clubs, employment, or personal development. Which areas give you the greatest sense of personal strength? Which areas give you the least? What can you do to find more satisfaction in your activities? Are you using fair standards in measuring your accomplishments?

Give yourself credit for the things you do well. Learn to feel good about yourself in these areas, regardless of what they may be. Think about the areas in which you make the least accomplishments. Do you really need to be an expert in these activities? Does less-than-perfect skill work just as well? If you have no reason to do certain things expertly, don't put yourself down. Some things are just not worth perfection. You may know someone who irons her dustcloths, but that doesn't mean you have to! Some ministers' wives have glowing talents in art or music, but you're no less a gift to the church without them. A story is told about a man who had almost superhuman strength. He concentrated so much on using great power that he often failed in simple tasks needing a light touch. Put your skills in perspective with what you need to do.

If you'd like to increase your skills in certain areas, see what steps need to be taken to bring this about. Do you need more information, training, practice, or encouragement in doing certain things? If so, who can help you? What opportunities are available for gaining needed skills? Set some specific goals that you can follow in making achievements.

Enjoy and appreciate the skills you have. Let this good feeling balance areas in which you feel less capable.

• *Control.*—Review areas in which you have a sense of choice or control. Which areas seem more restrictive: home, church, social groups, employment, or the like? Which areas affirm your ability to make good suggestions or have

positive influence on the group? What reward, honor, or recognition would increase your feeling of satisfaction? What would be needed to open up more options for you in decision making?

Lack of options can create a sense of helplessness in coping with daily concerns. But having to control every detail of every event can be just as stressful. Positive esteem does not require getting your way all the time or controlling everything that goes on around you. Decide how much control or influence you need to exert in order to feel good about yourself. If you need an excessive amount, perhaps a look at your self-concept would be helpful. Check to see if you expect every act to be approved or every deed applauded before feeling assured about yourself. If so, you may be measuring worth only in terms of personal triumphs or power to call all the shots. This way of measuring worth fails to take in all the ways of gaining esteem.

If you would like more influence, check out how you come across as a person. Do you state your ideas clearly and simply? Do you listen attentively to what others have to say? Do you let others express opinions and respect their rights? Can you gather facts and focus on the problem at hand? Can you enjoy being part of a group without dominating it? Positive esteem enables you to work with others without having to control them. Good relationships require a lot of give-and-take. When you feel good about your own worth, you can let others take the lead without feeling threatened. When your suggestions don't get adopted, you can avoid feeling rejected as a person.

• *Relationships.*—All persons do not need the same degree of closeness and affection. However, all of us need to feel loved and valued by others. Try to decide how close you need to be to people in order to feel valued as a person. Look at ways you respond to others. How do you show concern, interest, care, approval, or acceptance of others? Your need for closeness and your way of responding give valuable clues about relationship skills.

If you would like to feel more affection or acceptance, try to determine how open you are to others. In what ways do loved ones or friends show that they care about you as a person? How do you respond to them? Do you feel accepted for who you and what you are? What do you think keeps this acceptance from taking place? When you express a need, do you feel that friends or loved ones will try to meet it? How do you show concern or affection? Is it difficult for you to establish or keep up relationships? If you feel a real problem in this area, perhaps a trained counselor could help you identify your needs in relating to others. Understanding how you relate is important in all areas of life: marriage, family, career, social settings, and religious commitment.

• *Beliefs.*—Esteem grows out of acting upon your beliefs. Review the opportunities you have for expressing and acting on your convictions. Do you feel able to live up to your ethical ideals and religious commitment? Do you feel free to openly state your beliefs? Is your behavior consistent with your beliefs about honor, integrity, and morality? What standards do you use for deciding how to act? Do these standards reflect your deeply felt convictions?

Esteem also comes from seeing your beliefs and commitments honored by others. One of the joys of Christian fellowship is sharing commitment and religious teachings. Look for ways of strengthening your inner being through worship, service, and shared concern in the community of faith. Allow persons with spiritual wisdom to deepen your insights. Accept encouragement from those whose Christian character and example you admire. Take advantage of your role as a minister's wife to grow in understanding of faith at work in everyday situations.

Affirm your integrity as a person when your beliefs face a challenge. High esteem is not enhanced by rigid opinions or inflexible attitudes, but you will want to defend those core convictions upon which your faith rests. These basics of belief should contain eternal truth, the kind that stands the test of time and turmoil. Affirm in yourself that doubts and testing are not signs of spiritual failure.

The key to building self-esteem lies within yourself. Esteem is more than a pat on the back, but it does begin by affirming your worth as an individual. Drop negative approaches to wants and needs. Look beyond yourself to the possibilities God opens up before you. Look on self-esteem as a balance for crises, conflicts, and disappointments—and to keep things in perspective during high moments of success and victory.

### Realizing Self-Love

Self-love and self-centeredness are not the same. Self-love means making rational and positive choices about yourself—to grow, to expand your thinking, to mature mentally and spiritually, and to act in responsible ways. This kind of self-love allows you to see events and persons from a healthy perspective. Perhaps Christ had this kind of love in mind when He used self-love as the yardstick for measuring care for a neighbor (Matt. 19:19).

For the Christian, self-worth grows out of God's grace. His activity as Creator and Redeemer lays the foundation on which true worth is built. This approach to self-love is positive and healthy. God made you in His own image (Gen. 1:26). He chose you for fellowship with Him. He blessed you with the capacity to become His instrument in the world. Even when sin marred your fellowship with God, He didn't reject or cease loving you. Rather, He provided the way for you to be restored to a right relationship. He made you a new creature through Christ (2 Cor. 5:17). His Spirit equips you to fulfill a role in His kingdom (1 Cor. 12:4-7).

You can make self-worth a reality by reflecting God's love and presence at work in you. There's no better way to present a positive self-image than by becoming the person God created you to be. That's loving yourself the best way of all.

### Time Out

In what ways do you present a positive self-image as you go about daily tasks?

What areas of your personhood cause you the most concern?

*Take time to meet yourself, as though you were a stranger. Then take another look through God's eyes:*

Dear Father, my Creator, who knows me as no one else, help me see myself as a child of Your love. Show me how to live redemptively within my humanity as You did through Your Son, Jesus Christ, who lived in human form and felt our needs.

# 4

# Balancing Ministry and Home

*Joan watched TV a while, put the kids to bed, thumbed listlessly through a magazine, and finally went to bed. This was the third night in a row Todd had stayed at the church past ten o'clock. For the past two months Joan had seen less of him than when he served in the army. The kids couldn't understand the skipped family outings. Joan could count their special times together as a couple at about zero. Todd faced a lot of pressure from the church right now. Joan realized how sensitive he was to anything remotely resembling criticism, so she hated to add her gripes to his heavy load. But she was hurting too. She felt as though they were running on separate tracks, and that one day the tracks might never cross again. "I hate this life," Joan sobbed into her pillow. "I wish I'd known what it would be like married to a minister. I'd have said no."*

Does Joan's experience sound like the plot line in a soap opera? Think she's overreacting? Maybe so, but there's a cry for help in what she said. Many ministers' wives make that same cry. Some decide they don't want to put up with clergy life and move out, as rising divorce rates among ministers tell us. Others struggle along in silent pain because they can't cope with too little too often too long. Still other ministers' mates manage to tackle ministry demands with grace and great success. What makes the difference?

Balancing ministry and home is as much a philosophy of life as a series of dos and don'ts. A balanced outlook puts ministry into perspective as one part of a whole life committed to God's purpose. Marriage can then take its place as a sacred union and not as a sideline to ministry. Family life fulfills its purpose of lov-

ing support when not drained of meaning by absent, overstressed parents.

Balancing ministry and home really begins by deciding what part each needs to play in your life. Does ministry dominate every aspect of life or simply provide focus and direction? Do family ties override ministry responsibilities or serve to keep you in touch with needs of all the families in your ministry setting? In short, take some time to put ministry demands into perspective with other valid needs in your life.

## Responding to Family Pressures

What is there about ministry that often creates chaos in marriage and family life? For one thing, ministry tends to leave both emotional and economic security up for grabs. Few other occupations, with the possible exception of entertainers and professional athletes, are judged on high performance levels plus public appeal as are ministers. Ministers can get locked into the notion that they've got to please everyone and rush around showing how busy they are about the Lord's business. For another thing, few if any other occupations call for such deep personal commitment from wife and family as does ministry. By comparison, who cares if a lawyer's wife knows anything about law? Who takes notice if a doctor's child has a cold? Who keeps track of how regularly the coach's wife attends pep rallies, games, practice sessions, and booster club meetings? You get the picture.

Almost every survey of clergy couples turns up similar lists of demands: time pressure, expectations of perfection in marriage and family life, loneliness, endless routine of ministry events, lack of privacy, financial strain, church conflict, fear of being fired, and so on. Such pressures "go with the territory" in ministry. Getting rid of these demands doesn't seem possible or even desirable. So where do we go from here? Try sneaking up on the problem from another angle—get your marriage in tip-top shape. With that vital support in place you can be a good parent. You can take ministry demands in stride so that they lose some of their power to do harm.

### Maintaining Marriage Ideals

Counselors who work with troubled clergy couples often find a starving relationship. Some couples are out of touch with one another almost to the point of being strangers. They've neglected the bonds that make them a couple. They've lost sight of the mutual dreams that led them to marry in the first place. Losing touch is not difficult in a vocation that often robs one or both partners of emotional, intellectual, and spiritual resources and leaves little time to recover.

A constant drain on inner resources soon takes its toll on the marriage relationship. Some clergy wives describe their marriage as empty, boring, or irritating. Some ministry situations do seem like living in a pressure cooker. Pressure is not all bad, but you do need to be able to turn down the heat and regulate the steam to keep the lid from blowing off.

Maintaining a solid, loving marriage helps you adjust ministry pressure on your home life.

The goal of a good marriage is two people becoming one. The process calls for a mutual investment of self. Many barriers can crop up to hinder oneness. Usually, however, if a few basic trouble spots can be cleared up, the rest will be a lot easier to handle. These troublesome spots revolve around communication, emotions, conflict, and intimacy.

### Clearing Up Communication

Communication simply means exchanging meaning with someone else. This exchange can take a variety of forms: words, tone of voice, gestures, facial expression, touching, and so on. Failure to communicate is virtually impossible. A popular idea holds that no communication takes place unless you agree or understand each other. That idea is not true. Meaning has been exchanged even if you're misunderstood or ignored. Clear communication, though, needs some special care:

- freedom to speak
- trust
- mutual respect for feelings
- willingness to listen and hear

Clear communication thrives on freedom to say what's on your mind. Many marriage partners grew up in a home where opinions were kept inside, talk was dominated by one per-

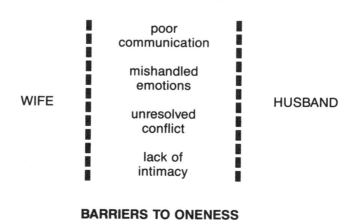

WIFE                    poor
                   communication          HUSBAND

                    mishandled
                    emotions

                    unresolved
                    conflict

                    lack of
                    intimacy

**BARRIERS TO ONENESS**

son, or topics were limited to the weather, sports, and the like. These partners often won't feel free to share inmost thoughts. In fact, they may not even know how to verbalize ideas very easily. They may become uncomfortable, change the subject, or leave when the talk gets too personal. If you or your husband have this difficulty, give yourselves permission to speak openly with each other. Assure each other that talking about feelings, fears, needs, and hopes out loud is better than keeping them locked inside. Promise each other patience when words don't come out easily or may seem harsh. Giving one another freedom to speak takes a lot of the anxiety out of relationships—never knowing what each of you think about things.

Even if you have freedom to speak, a sense of trust will be essential to sharing at more than a surface level. Opening up your inmost feelings makes you vulnerable to your hearer. Fears about rejection, criticism, or attack often block tries at sharing. In addition, you need the assurance that confidences will be kept between you. Assure each other of willingness to hear what is said without using it as emotional blackmail later. Agree to speak frankly, to disagree, and to level with each other without fear of reprisal. Communicating without this sense of trust will never go beyond passing along facts at best or playing psychological games at worst.

Expressing feelings openly is often hard to do, but *hearing* them can be equally tough. Intense or negative feelings are especially rough to hear and deal with. Practice sharing ordinary feelings so that the intense ones don't get bottled up and burst loose all at once. Try using "I" statements instead of "they," "it," or "you." For example: "I think the color looks too dark," instead of: "You can never tell about colors." Or: "I get nervous when we come here," instead of "This place is creepy." "I" statements state what you think or feel better than vague, impersonal observations. Don't assume your husband reads your mind and knows what you mean by subtle hints or hidden messages.

Expressing feelings may be easier for you than for your husband. Our macho-biased culture tends to idolize the strong, silent types who grit their teeth and hide feelings. Also, myths about ministry spread the idea that ministers never have strong feelings about things, never get angry, never need to explode with rage over stupidity like anyone else. One minister's wife got upset because her husband expressed so much anger. She felt threatened by his outbursts, even though the anger was not aimed at her. She failed to realize that her husband felt free to vent his anger only with her. Work at respecting feelings. Denying or belittling feelings only makes them more difficult to handle. You don't have to agree with each other's feelings—only to accept the right to have and express them.

Spouses often complain: "You haven't heard a word I've said!" The accusation is often true. Words quite literally went in one ear and out the other. Clear communication requires both speaker and listener to take part in the exchange. Good listening means paying attention, thinking about what is said, noting feelings, and encouraging the speaker's attempts at sharing. This kind of listening involves a risk, for you might hear something unpleasant or critical. But good listening is a great way to discover real needs, to understand the speaker, and to show your concern. Good listening is more than processing words; it means responding to the whole message, spoken or implied.

Loving communication really builds a solid support for marriage relationships. For one thing, you don't have to fear a disagreement. You can talk issues out. You won't have to hide feelings. Pressures and stresses can be named without pushing you apart. Tension lessens when talking doesn't end in browbeating, threats, rejection, and sulking. Open lines of communication give a sense of security to your relationship.

### Getting in Touch with Feelings

Feelings are your inner assessment of what's going on. They start as a physical reaction, then get processed by the nervous system and brain. Feelings may stay at a subconscious

**TALK THAT HURTS**

| | | |
|---|---|---|
| ▼ interrupting | ▼ crudeness | ▼ hogging the conversation |
| ▼ correcting | ▼ disrespect | |
| ▼ nagging | ▼ vulgarity | ▼ putting mate down in front of others |
| ▼ name calling | ▼ withholding praise | |
| ▼ belittling | ▼ dishonesty | ▼ dragging up old feuds or failures in the past |
| ▼ sarcasm | ▼ insults | |

level or get formed into thoughts. This process is both natural and automatic. You have no control over feelings taking place. However, you do control how you interpret and act on feelings.

Feelings are neither moral nor immoral because of their physical origins. Having any kind of feeling is not sinful. Morality comes into play when you give meaning to feelings and express them outwardly. Many feelings get labeled as bad or unacceptable for Christians. All feelings, though, underlie everything you say or do. Denying them just mishandles the good purpose God created feelings to give us.

You may not always identify the feelings you experience. You may be unaware that you come across as angry, anxious, sad, or embarrassed at times. In fact, you might be hiding your true feelings from yourself if you suspect they might be "wrong" ones. Notice how you show joy, affection, anger, fear, gratitude, sadness, sensuality, guilt, or worry. Do you know for sure how your husband expresses these feelings? Usually each person uses a variety of signals to reveal emotions. Some signs to watch are tone of voice, facial expressions, body position, word choice, too much talking, no talking, gestures, and similar unspoken cues. In fact, body language often tells more about feelings than do spoken words.

Think about the way you react when feelings come out. Can you deal with most feelings comfortably? Do you attempt to deny or explain feelings away: "No, you aren't angry—you're just a little tired right now." Anger or any other feeling is very real to the one experiencing it. You can help deal with feelings by your response to them: "I sense that you're unhappy (angry, worried, anxious, or whatever the feeling may be). If so, I'd like to know so we can do something about it."

Work at making it safe to express feelings in your marriage. When listening to feelings, don't try to give logical explanations or interpretations. Just listen. Gradually build trust toward sharing very tender feelings. Don't prod or pump for more than the other is ready to share. Above all, don't assume you know each other's feelings automatically. If in doubt, ask. "So you feel happy about this?" or, "I hear you saying that you're angry about my extra work load." Checking out feelings lets both of you clear the air. Mistaken ideas can be mended. Feeling understood can heal a lot of mental anguish.

Getting in touch with feelings can prevent frustration, isolation, and guessing games in your relationship. You can get at the root of issues, find out dreams, and know for sure what pleases, fulfills, and helps each other.

## Resolving Conflict

Some marriages fall apart after the first serious argument. The couples simply couldn't deal with conflicts in an appropriate way. Some of these couples probably believed that any disagreement at all meant love had ended. Love isn't built on agreement so much as on commitment to do the best for each other individually and as a couple. Love plays a part in handling conflict but, by itself, is not enough.

People usually deal with conflict in a few basic ways. Look through the following list of conflict responses and note the way you *most often* choose:

- Deny any problem exists.
- Leave the scene.
- Try to smooth everything over.
- Take charge and impose your will.
- Give in enough to make peace.
- Work out a mutually satisfactory solution.

Any of these responses can work, provided the problem goes away. But all except the last response leave gaps in the relationship. Bridging the gaps, however, is essential for a long-term, satisfying relationship. The process requires openness, trust, patience, and willingness to work at it and work at it and work at it. Quick fixes just don't do the trick!

Conflict can actually strengthen marriage when handled in a healthy way. Working out disagreements can lead to the discovery of more options and creative solutions. Conflict has the potential for both good and ill. You can use it so that good takes place.

*1. Name the cause of conflict.*—What's causing the disagreement: differing opinions, methods, or goals?

*2. Attack the problem rather than each other.*— Insults, accusations, and threats add nothing but grief to the process. For example, if you're debating the purchase of a new sofa, confine remarks to the sofa's merits and not to the character of the one who wants to buy it. Rejecting an idea doesn't mean rejecting the person who thought it. Zeroing in on each other attacks self-esteem. Self-defensive tactics then go into action and settling the issue gets lost. Take responsibility for your part in focusing on the issue without name-calling, sulking, or hitting below the belt.

*3. Hear all sides of the problem.*—Get the facts in order. Give each other equal time for uninterrupted statements of opinion about the matter. Resist butting in with corrections or counterarguments. Even if you win your point, you may lose the chance of settling the bigger issue.

*4. Underscore points of agreement.*—Few conflicts are totally without some common ground. You may have a common goal even if methods of getting there differ. Use this point of agreement as the basis of settling the dispute. For example, both may want a new sofa, but one wants a sleeper and the other insists on a sectional grouping. The sofa's not the issue here—rather, the kind. Follow up by deciding what you really want most, what you identify as priorities.

*5. State the options.*—Most problems have any number of workable solutions. List as many as possible. What alternatives to your present view would you be willing to accept? What seems best for both of you in the long run?

*6. Agree on a solution.*—Settle who does what and when. If no solution is possible right now, agree on what you *can* do about the problem: drop the subject, get more facts, discuss it later if new options come up. The point is to let the argument end when the time comes. Avoid dragging it out or saving this conflict as fuel for the next disagreement.

Agreeing to disagree takes a lot of pressure off day-to-day decisions. Settling disputes makes future ones less threatening. You can choose not to pursue any conflict if it causes more pain than gain. But learn to choose together.

## Cultivating Intimacy

Intimacy in marriage often brings to mind the sexual part of the relationship. However, intimacy really includes many kinds of closeness. It has to do with mutual fulfillment in all areas of shared living. Howard and Charlotte Clinebell suggest that intimacy includes emotions, ideas, aesthetics, creative activities, recreation, work, crises, conflict, shared commitment, and spiritual concerns, as well as sexual union.

Soon after the honeymoon most couples discover that intimacy has to mean more than sex for the marriage to deepen and endure. A kind of closeness needs to develop that will help the marriage through the worse, sickness, and poorer clauses of the wedding vows. Intimacy can be found if both partners want it and work persistently to achieve it. A familiar but accurate symbol for marriage is a garden that needs daily tending to flourish.

Some areas of your marriage relationship may seem less comfortable or satisfying to you. These areas are potential growth points as a couple. Think about what you'd like to see happen in these areas. Check these feelings with your husband, and then look for some specific ways you can deepen intimacy in needy areas. Be on the lookout for barriers that may be hindering closeness.

Many couples are unaware of each other's feelings about their marriage. It is not unusual for one spouse to feel perfectly contented while the other needs or wants to see some changes take place. If that is your case, tactfully and gently suggest what you feel to be

steps in the right direction. Some mates avoid exploring their relationship for fear they'll be unable to handle any needs, wants, or problems they uncover. Areas of need, however, don't indicate a failed relationship, only one in need of some extra attention to make it super good.

Consider some of these factors that deepen intimacy:

• *Time.*—A myth has grown up around providing *quality* time in relationships, as though a few minutes of intense sharing every now and then will do the trick. *Quantity* of time is essential in building quality relationships. Regular times of quiet, privacy, and mutual enjoyment are needed. These times can come through walks, short trips, quiet evenings, favorite recreational activities, hobbies, dining out, or any kind of special pleasures you share. Make it a point to set aside the time and honor this appointment as you would any other. Undergird the strong ties in your marriage so you can rely on that strength during the rough times.

• *Awareness.*—Open-eyed sensitivity is crucial in good marriages. Many couples simply don't pay attention to what's happening between them. Think about the pressures each of you are under: work load, health, child care, fi-

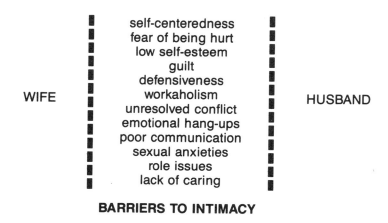

WIFE                                                                HUSBAND

self-centeredness
fear of being hurt
low self-esteem
guilt
defensiveness
workaholism
unresolved conflict
emotional hang-ups
poor communication
sexual anxieties
role issues
lack of caring

**BARRIERS TO INTIMACY**

nances, emotional upheavals, and other daily demands. Realize that such things affect all areas of your relationship.

Make the effort to find out who you are as persons. Appreciate and affirm the differences as well as similarities. Trace how these personal attributes work out in your relationship. Learn the unspoken cues and subtle nuances that reveal feelings. Tune in to the silent message implied in mood, appearance, and behavior. Sensitive mates come to know when the other needs a hug or pat on the back.

• *Love.*—Every marriage sparkles when romance is alive and well. But there's always a need for the kind of love that bears, believes, hopes, and endures all things. Renew the commitment that drew you together as a couple. Find ways of showing that you care deeply about each other, that you need each other. A frequent omission is *saying* that you love your mate. Showing love is wonderful, but hearing it is special.

Sex is not the same as love, but it is an extension of love. Deepening sexual intimacy doesn't mean setting aside personal needs in exchange for the physical gymnastics often advocated in popular novels or marriage manuals. A more satisfying approach is to find out what satisfies, fulfills, and affirms each other as a person as well as a sexual being. Learning to communicate sexual needs greatly aids sexual harmony. If you feel inhibited or afraid your comments may be misinterpreted, start by praising those expressions of sexual intimacy you can openly discuss. Let this level of sharing pave the way to deeper insights. Share a reliable book or article that says what you'd like to: "This is what I mean but can't say too well. What do you feel about it?" Take advantage of minister-mate seminars or marriage enrichment retreats that provide an encouraging atmosphere for discussing relationships in a nonthreatening way.

Take some of the pressure off your sexual relationship by making sure it's not the only kind of intimacy you share. A lot of the time you'll need a good friend more than a lover. Cultivate all areas of life together so that your total relationship is balanced. Sexual needs or problems can best be mended when the rest of your relationship is healthy and growing.

The New Testament places marriage under the lordship of Jesus Christ, and He set it in the context of fulfilling God's purpose: "Haven't you read the scripture that says that in the beginning the Creator made people male and female? And God said, 'For this reason a man will leave his father and mother and unite with his wife, and the two will become one'" (Matt. 19:4-5). Marriage is to be part of a life-style that reflects God's intention, a mutual submission in love to carry out God's plan. This applies to ministers and their wives just like anyone else. Marriage is not meant to pay the price of misplaced ministry aims.

Coming together as one can't fully or perhaps rightly be judged by tradition, cultural styles, or social standards—certainly not by phony ideals of what clergy couples are "supposed" to be like. The true measure of your marriage relationship lies in fulfilling God's purpose along whatever paths His revealed will takes you. Oneness won't come from adopting the latest fad in male/female roles or clinging without question to parental example. Oneness is God's gift, part of the mystery of the working of His Spirit within you (Eph. 5:32).

## For the Children's Sake

Parents in ministry face all the challenges most families encounter. But they also come up against a few subtle, perhaps unique tests in a ministry setting that are not typical to most homes. Family life for ministers has a way of getting deeply entwined with church activities. Sometimes the line between ministry goals and family identity becomes blurred.

Parenting in ministry is not an either/or situation but a both/and arena. The New Testament places a lot of importance on family life for church leaders: "able to manage his own family well and make his children obey him with all respect. For if a man does not know how to manage his own family, how can he take care of the church of God?" (1 Tim. 3:4-5).

Knowing the proper place of family is essential in setting ministry priorities. Family time does not keep any minister from "doing ministry." Family life is very much a part of ministering. One cannot be done at the expense of the other. This delicate balancing act may have been one reason the apostle Paul urged ministers to weigh the impact of marriage on Christian service (1 Cor. 7:32-35). Marriage vows are no less sacred than vocational ones.

**Setting Parenting Priorities**

Family life needs a share of time. Family needs give the best clues in setting priorities on time use. For example, parents of infants naturally have to give more attention to feeding, dressing, bathing, and watching over the baby. Less attention in these areas would be needed for teens. Teens, in turn, need more one-on-one exchanges about principles, ethics, or dealing with situations they face outside the home. Work out family time that meets your children's needs. If you have a new baby in the house, a sick child, or a teen going through a rough period, don't invest so much time in church activities. Be there for your child. Trying to carry out church activities as though a child makes no difference is ridiculous. A music minister's wife collapsed from exhaustion while trying to play piano for her husband's five choirs and at the same time tend to a fussy six-month-old son.

At times the family's needs will have to take first place. At other times ministry demands will rank higher. If you tend to family needs with integrity, the family won't begrudge you the time for ministry concerns. If, however, the family always gets the short end of the stick, they will resent ministry's claims on their lives. It is sad to hear a minister's child, now in her fifties, recall: "There was so much love for the church in our house that there seemed to be very little left over for my brother and me."

Many of the skills in communication, expressing feelings, resolving conflict, and developing closeness can be applied to parenting. You might want to review these topics with an eye to their use in strengthening your parenting skills.

**Affirming Your Children**

Children of ministers need to be accepted as persons in their own right and not merely as extensions of that ministry. Clergy couples sometimes expect their children to be living proof of their theology, commitment, or ministry authority. Ministers can be tempted into substituting service goals for family goals as though they were one and the same. Children reared under these conditions often seem like just another ministry program to take charge of and shape up.

Each child is born with a unique temperament and potential. Each child needs to be free to develop at his or her own pace. Nowhere is this need more critical than in ministry families. Clergy children often face so many expectations about their behavior, leadership, and personality. What if that child is shy or mischievous or not particularly talented? How will these children set their own pace when they are thrust so often into adult responsibilities or made to "grow up" too soon?

Help your children deal with issues they face in a ministry setting. Take time to explain what ministry means. Discuss the beliefs and principles your family lives by. Avoid imposing rules on your children simply because they are "the minister's kids." Share your faith with them through action as well as verbal teachings.

Watch for signs that ministry demands may be too much for your children to handle. Tension, irritability, fatigue, and apathy are often signals of stress. Pull back from so much going—every meeting can't be that crucial. Is your own desire to please everyone leading to overinvolvement for the family? Are you putting pressure on your children to take more responsibility in the church or to be more spiritually mature than they can handle?

Above all, avoid setting your children up as examples. All Christians should be examples in a sense, but that is a personal commitment growing out of spiritual maturity; it should not be a rule imposed on a child for ministry's sake. Your children have no more responsibility in being an example than any other child their age.

**Sharing Family Joy**

Ministry offers many good things to families: travel, loving church friends, meeting interesting people, sharing religious faith, and helping others. These benefits are often lacking in today's family emphasis on success and material possessions. Rejoice in the good things with your children. A lot of their attitude toward God, the church, and faith will be picked up from your attitude toward ministry. Let them see the blessings as well as the testings.

Love for God and for His purpose in the world is the greatest heritage you can pass on to your children. They will treasure this heritage provided they don't become sacrifices to your ministry goals or personal ambition.

**Time Out**

What part of your marriage and family life needs most attention now?

What change would you like to see take place in this area of concern? What benefits, strengths, or helps can you draw from your ministry setting to bring about the desired change?

*Mentally review your marriage and family history, as though reading about it in a magazine. Celebrate the adventure, the good times and the bad. Then lift them up to God:*

Dear Father: we became a couple, a family, as part of Your purpose. Show us how to live in Your grace so that we can enjoy our days, loving and forgiving each other as You did through Jesus Christ.

# 5

# Making the Most of Stress

*"This week has been the pits," Joan muttered as she settled Jeremy in his car seat for another trip to the church. "Getting this family on the road is like moving a circus." Todd had raced off earlier to the men's pancake supper, leaving Joan to round up the kids. That was no small chore. Mark, their oldest, resented leaving his soccer game early. Five-year-old Annie refused to have her hair brushed, and Joan was too tired to fuss with her. Only baby Jeremy seemed content, but even he fussed all week because of the extra night meetings. Budget planning, a guest missionary speaker, the youth awards banquet, and a church growth rally all landed in one week on top of her turn to work in the community clothes closet. "All I need," thought Joan, "is a broken leg, and the week will be perfect!"*

How would you describe Joan's week: typical, no big deal, a big headache, stressful? *Stressful* is a word that quickly comes to mind. *Stress* is a handy catchword nowadays for all the hassles that come along. Joan, however, is the only one who can decide if her week was truly stressful. Why? Because stress is *her response* to the demands made on her. Her opin-

ion of the week could range all the way from exhilarating to depressing, depending on how she looks at her job load.

That's right—stress is your view of the situation, not the situation itself. Your outlook can change though the situation may not. Dealing with your outlook, then, is the key to coping with stress. No one denies that ministers' wives have plenty of demands made on them. The real question concerns ways of managing stress so that it works for good instead of harm.

Let's look at some typical stress-provoking factors that ministry families face. See how these factors work out in your daily routine. Stress is not all bad and, in fact, serves a very healthy purpose. You may be overlooking this "good stress" benefit in facing your demands.

## Signs of Stress

Dr. Hans Selye pioneered the study of human stress. In fact, he borrowed the word *stress* from physics where it referred to a force pressing on, twisting, or straining an object. He applied this idea of stress to the physical, chemical, and emotional factors that cause ten-

| STRESSORS | RESPONSE | STRESS LEVEL |
|---|---|---|
| (factors making demands on body, mind, or emotions) →→→→→ | (personal view of stressors and reaction to them) →→→→→ | (degree of good or harmful effects felt in responding) |

**ELEMENTS IN STRESS**

sion in human beings. Twisting a paper clip soon causes metal fatigue so that it breaks. Continual tension in human beings also causes fatigue and can lead to serious illness, even death. Stress, then, needs to be taken seriously but also correctly understood.

Stress can be tricky in that not everyone responds to stressors in the same way. Demands that floor one person often excite and challenge someone else. For example, speaking before a large group petrifies some people, while others love the idea and enjoy appearing before an audience. The task is the same, so the difference must lie in how each person reacts to it. Each person responds to stressors in his or her own way. Some persons can take on many demands at once with little or no pressure. Others, however, can cope with only one or two demands at a time. Opposites, in fact, sometimes marry! The husband can be whizzing around tending to a dozen things while his wife gets a headache trying to keep up with him. Each couple needs to understand each other's stress limits. Failure to deal with very different stress responses usually leads to tension in living or trying to work together—one spouse rushing ahead, the other pulling back. Understanding your own and your mate's optimum stress level can help you balance your way of sharing tasks. The one of you needing a higher activity level to feel good can take on more demands without trying to place the same load on the other spouse.

Your stress level shows up in some fairly clear signals. Good stress levels—demands not exceeding your capacity to cope—give you a sense of self-control, energy, challenge, motivation, and that "good tired" feeling when tasks are done. Harmful stress levels—demands exceeding your capacity to cope—can result in irritability, anxiety, boredom, endless fatigue, depression, and all kinds of physical ailments ranging from colds and allergies to heart attacks.

Some physical signs you can look for when stress levels get too high are: dizziness, weakness, trembling, sweating, dry mouth and throat, insomnia, frequent urination, diarrhea, indigestion, queasiness, headaches,

backaches, missed menstrual cycles, and feeling nervous or "keyed up" all the time. Not all of these signs come from stress, to be sure, but a regular pattern of them may mean that demands are giving you an overload. Like an electrical outlet with too many appliances plugged in, you may be facing an energy drain or a blowout.

Some behaviors that indicate high stress levels are: lack of concentration, irritability, unexplained urges to cry or hide, nervous laughter, increased use of medicines, accident proneness, and restlessness. An unusual or unaccounted for number of these behaviors can point to stress.

You can't avoid stress. The alternative to stress, like aging, is death. Even during sleep your body takes care of some demands by functioning. So the approach to coping with stress is not to do away with demands. Rather, cope by locating your stressors, determining the level you can best handle, and finding ways of keeping demands within that level. Managing stress is like tuning a violin. The strings need the right amount of tension to play on pitch and in harmony with other instruments. Too much or too little tension creates a problem in the orchestra, and too many or too few stressors do the same in your life.

### Identifying Stressors

Ministers' stress gets a good bit of attention these days. Survey responses from ministers of all denominations reveal stress in areas of time management, role expectations, high performance demands, lack of family time, dealing with guilt and anger, and fear of criticism. These stressors became even more intense if coupled with financial strain, church conflicts, frequent career moves, and inadequate retirement funds. When ministers' wives were surveyed, they voiced similar concerns. Wives, however, added some special stressors they faced: loneliness, isolation, inner conflicts, and spiritual stagnation. All the surveys show that an average clergy couple deals with some stress.

Many of the typical stressors fall into four main groups: role expectations, church rela-

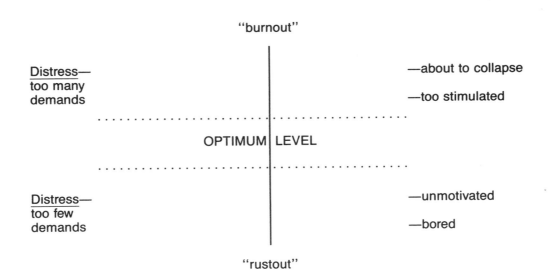

"burnout"

Distress— too many demands

—about to collapse

—too stimulated

OPTIMUM LEVEL

Distress— too few demands

—unmotivated

—bored

"rustout"

**LOCATING YOUR OPTIMUM STRESS LEVEL**

tionships, family relationships, and spiritual concerns. Spotting your stressors in these broad areas often sheds light on a wide range of problems. Demands often overlap, and stressors may have a common source. Check for stressors you face in this overview of typical demands.

### Role Expectations

Role expectations have to do with ideas about your proper place in the scheme of things. You deal with these expectations on two levels: as a woman and as a minister's wife. At this point in American culture, opinions about appropriate sex roles for men and women are changing. The women's movement and the quest for personal fulfillment upset old standards of how men and women should view themselves in relation to society. Your approach to marriage, family life, and career goals often directly reflects how you see yourself as a person. Let's examine some ways role expectations show up in your ministry setting.

Serving as a minister's wife gives you an overlapping pattern of expectations. First, you have an opinion of what ministry should be. You also have ideals about your husband as a mate and as a minister. Moreover, you probably have an idea of how you'd like to live as mate and as minister's wife too. Guess what— you're not the only one with a set of ideas on the subject! Your husband has his opinion, as does the ministry field he serves, about you and your role. If all three areas have similar expectations, you can probably count on a fairly satisfying relationship between yourself, your spouse, and his ministry. Where expectations clash, however, you are likely to feel some degree of stress. We've already looked at ways of learning congregational expectations (chaps. 1 and 2). Using these guidelines, compare what you perceive to be ministry expectations of you with your own ideas about serving.

Find out what your husband expects of you as a wife and as part of his ministry. For example, ask him what activities on your part fit most comfortably with his aims, personality, and ministry style. He may feel more secure if you keep a low profile in his ministry setting. Surveys show that some ministers see less

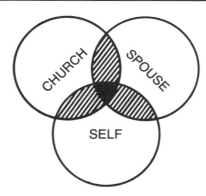

**POTENTIAL PRESSURE POINTS
IN AREAS OF SHARED ROLE EXPECTATIONS**

need for a spouse's involvement in church activities than their wives do. Some ministers feel uneasy about a wife who wants to be "co-pastor." Other ministers feel threatened if their wife seems to be a better or more popular church leader. Your husband's self-esteem can be undercut if he feels you're competing with him. You've probably heard comments about ministers' wives that hint at this kind of situation: she writes his sermons, she makes him look good, he can keep a church only because she does the work, and so on. Such remarks often go beyond good-humored joking.

Many ministers' wives feel pressured to do more in church than they really would like. If you share this concern, try to find out why you feel that way. What do you expect of yourself as a minister's wife? Recall how you came to those conclusions. What factors influenced your thinking? Have you set unrealistic goals for yourself? Have you let past experience in the church, the example of other ministers' wives, books, or denominational role models put pressure on you to act a certain way? Have you projected your own ideals onto your husband or his ministry field? Have you misinterpreted your sense of commitment as it applies to your role as a minister's wife? These inner forces may be causing stress as you measure your effectiveness as woman, mate, and minister's wife.

About half of all ministers' wives work outside the home. Many of these do so because the family needs the income to get by. Many ministers are bivocational. Both spouses' career demands, plus ministry responsibilities, can be stressful. Two-income, especially two-clergy, households often face conflict over work loads as well as family responsibilities. Keeping up traditional views of home and marriage along with career goals often drains women of physical and emotional strength. Your husband may agree to your working, but he may not agree to take on extra chores, child care, or adjustments in his own schedule because of your job. He may resent the demands your job makes on your time or the attention your career takes away from him. A clash may come over whose career gets first priority in moves, education, time management, and the like.

Congregations tend to see the minister's marriage in a traditional patriarchal pattern of male breadwinner, female homemaker. Many couples, however, may wish to live by less traditional patterns, deciding tasks according to interests, abilities, or needs. More and more clergy wives have seminary training or professional degrees. Many of these women feel a call to ministry in their own right. Still other wives simply want a different life-style than traditional role models offer. If you see yourself in a nontraditional role, take into account some added stressors. Many husbands and congregations, though often sympathetic to a wife's career desires, still hold to old standards. Letting go of these ideals may not be easy.

Identifying preferred roles in your marriage involves finding out what each of you expect of each other. Both of you may share similar ideas, but you may also differ about appropriate sex roles, career choices, and family lifestyle. Determine your priorities for your marriage and for yourself as a person. Compare these two priority areas. Just how realistic are your goals in the light of building a sound marriage? Weigh the impact your goals have on your wider responsibilities as a mate.

Two-clergy couples have the task of separating ministry roles from their spouse and parent roles. Some couples identify so completely with ministry tasks that they bring "church" home with them. They may relate almost entirely minister-to-minister rather than spouse-to-spouse. They sometimes carry professional conflicts into private life. Competition, ambition, and opinions of each other's competence can make for strained relationships at home. Stress builds up when both spouses give too much of themselves to vocational goals and too little to each other as persons or as a couple.

Review your expectations and get some idea about what each of you want and need from ministry. Work toward defining a mutually fulfilling role for you as part of that ministry.

### Church Relationships

No matter how anonymous you might like to be, you'll never get by as "just another member" of your husband's congregation. You'll be highly visible and most likely looked on as an expert in religious matters. This public image often creates stress in social relationships as well as in church activities.

People often feel hesitant about expressing their feelings directly to a minister. They feel less threatened, however, in speaking to the minister's wife. So you'll probably be singled out to carry messages to your husband. This request may be a direct one, but often it is a subtle, indirect hint. Subjects may be discussed in your presence with the hope you'll repeat them to your husband later. Or, you may be told "someone" was not happy about a church matter, just a friendly "reminder" to pass on. Stress comes when you get caught in the crossfire between your husband and congregants. Conflict situations are especially uncomfortable when hearing your husband criticized. Using you as a messenger lets the speaker get out of responsibility for his or her words. You get stuck with the unpleasantness of both hearing and repeating the message. Check to see who may be using you this way. Redirect the message: "I'm sure my husband would like to talk this over with you. Shall I tell him you'll call?"

Lack of peer relationships in the church can give you a sense of isolation. You'll nearly always be seen as a "leader" or authority figure. This status gives you few opportunities to be yourself. Staying in the limelight gets tiring. You'll naturally be drawn to certain persons, enjoy the company of certain families more than others, and want to be close to these special ones. Tension comes in balancing your need for friendships with openness toward all congregants. Stress may become intense if you lack social outlets or must hide your friendships rather than offend. The other side of the coin can be equally distressing if congregants want to monopolize all your free time.

Many subtle pressures go along with ministry relationships. Age, economic, and cultural differences may vary widely between you and those on the ministry field. You may be living in the shadow of a former minister's wife who served in ways very different from your chosen role. Some church women may feel resentment or jealousy. At times you may be treated according to the amount of approval your husband's ministry has earned—greeted with open arms when he does well or shunned when he's out of favor. Your desire to please can push you into an endless round of speaking engagements, devotionals, club work, class meetings, or women's groups.

Try to get some idea of the stressors that may be growing out of ministry relationships.

Compare these stressful situations to what you'd like to see happening.

**Family Relationships**

Ministry concerns frequently spill over into family life. Ministry stressors tend to intensify any on-going problem areas in your private life. Marital or family conflict can color your outlook on ministry. Adjusting to a new baby, caring for a sick child, leaving a comfortable location, meeting needs of aged or ill parents, and working through marital issues are examples of common family stressors.

Finding family time can be a major concern. Some clergy families try to substitute time together at church events for private time. This practice works only at a very superficial level. Moreover, ministers' wives with jobs of their own face extra time drains. The congregation likely expects them to carry a full load of religious duties in addition to family and job responsibilities.

Many ministers' wives don't know how to express their needs to a husband already burdened by ministry concerns. Sometimes wives choose to swallow their hurts rather than confront their husband with them. How often have you wanted to talk over a problem only to find your husband exhausted by meetings, hospital calls, or counseling sessions? How can you get across your sense of loss when he may be battling an angry church committee, dissatisfied supervisor, or personal attack? You can quickly become a martyr to his serving. Keeping personal concerns to yourself, however, only increases their impact on your self-esteem. One partner cannot possibly bear the whole burden of social, intellectual, and spiritual support for the marriage; both need to be involved with each other's need.

Limited time as a family may lead to another kind of false solution to needs: focusing exclusively on the children. One pastor's wife complained, "When my husband comes in, he rushes to our boys. I get a peck on the cheek, but they get his full attention till bedtime. By then I'm exhausted, and my husband is in no mood for anything but TV." Placing the children at the center of the relationship robs couples of vital intimacy as marriage partners. It also robs children of realistic role models for marriage and parenting.

Disorganized, disruptive home life often sends ministers or their mates elsewhere to seek release. Ministers readily find excuses to escape unpleasant situations at home: a visit, office work, ministerial meetings, study—anything rather than deal with squabbles with wife or children. The attention and admiration provided by parishioners may be more satisfying than family relationships.

Try to pinpoint areas in family life that cause you concern. List the most difficult demands you face as a parent and spouse. Compare these with your desires for marriage and family life.

**Spiritual Concerns**

Who's your minister, the one who gives you pastoral care? Don't say your husband, for he's really not the ideal one for the job. This is one case where he can't be everything to everyone. Sometimes your husband and his ministry are the *cause* of your stress! Someone else needs to hear that hurt. You need spiritual growth in your own right. You may need a time of confession or guidance outside your husband's religious leadership. You need the kind of openness and affirmation a more neutral observer might provide. This is not to say that your husband can't give you spiritual guidance, inspiration, or encouragement. Rather, he may be too close to the situation.

Heavy involvement on the ministry field may leave your spiritual resources at low ebb. Continual feeding of others will not always feed you. You may find yourself needing someone outside your ministry setting to hear your feelings, accept you, and offer spiritual counsel. You certainly will benefit from a time of retreat and renewal to strengthen spiritual gifts and deepen your awareness of God's purpose in your life.

These four areas of concern touch on many parts of your life as a minister's wife. Perhaps you're aware of personal stressors not discussed here. Keep them in mind as you read through some coping techniques.

### Coping Skills

Coping with stress begins by accepting the fact that it's there. You will deal with stressors all your life. Doesn't it make you feel better just to know you're not alone in feeling the way you do about things? Also, don't forget that stress is normal and even helpful. Feelings of anxiety, discomfort, and tension serve to warn you that all is not well, that the time has come to make some adjustments in your daily routine.

The nature of stress gives some valuable clues in coping:

1. *Stress lies in you,* not in outside forces working on you. You create your own stress by how you respond to demands made on you.
2. *You can feel stressed by good things as well as unpleasant ones.* Pressure from too many happy events can be just as hard on you as from too many tough ones. For example, Christmas is one of the most stressful times in our society. Easter is a particularly tense time for those in ministry.
3. *A good level of stress can make life enjoyable.* Your day perks along at a pleasant pace most of the time.

The secret to managing stress lies in spacing out demands so you work at your optimum level. No matter what kind of stressors you face, some tried and proven coping methods do exist to lessen strain. Four basic ways of dealing with stress can give you more control over your responses:

- *Change your outlook.*—Try calling stressors by some other name.
- *Adjust your approach.*—Practice flexibility.
- *Weigh your options.*—Eliminate some "either-or's."
- *Build your resources.*—Be mentally, physically, and spiritually fit.

*Changing your outlook* on stress can transform it into opportunity, challenge, or motivator. The difference in your response can be amazing. It's the old "stepping stone or stumbling block" idea. You have the choice!

Keep track of change taking place in your marriage, family life, and ministry setting. Remind yourself that these times of adjustment tend to create more stress. Allow yourself extra time and leeway in dealing with them. Knowing that a speedbreaker lies across the street lets you approach it slowly and not get knocked into the windshield by running over it at full speed. The same principle works with stressors.

Don't take every negative word as a personal threat. People often speak or act without thinking. Look with a kind eye on your own shortcomings. Mistakes, even huge ones, are not the end of the world. A wise counselor once said, "One of the reasons ministers' wives have headaches is because their halos are too tight!" Being perfect in everything is not really helpful. Take off your Supergal suit and relax.

Avoid letting others set your agenda all the time. You can find yourself driven by your husband's whims, your children's reluctance to do for themselves, church members' criticism, or current fashions and fads. Find your own sense of purpose in the midst of others' needs. Do what seems needful, realizing you can't do everything.

Much is sacred about commitment to God's call, but not every ministry demand is sacred. Calling attention to your husband's unnecessary absences from home, irregular schedule, or overcommitment to ministry tasks may seem like fussing at God, but it is not. Make your genuine needs and concerns known. Be direct, clear, and firm about problems you need help in handling. You may get resistance at first, but you may also gain needed relief through persistence, tact, and gentle persuasion.

*Adjusting your approach* puts tasks in perspective. Pilots of airliners adjust their approach to match the situation on the landing strip. Try the same thing with stressful situations. Screaming is not always appropriate. Make a list of all the things you do in a typical week. Ask yourself about each: Do I need to do this at all? Can I do this occasionally rather than daily? Do I spend too much time on this? Do I try to do this perfectly each time when a "lick and a promise" would do just as well?

Choose your battles carefully. Some issues are not worth the fuss. Find out when it's good to retreat, surrender, or compromise. Losing a small battle doesn't always mean losing the larger issue. Affirm yourself when you do lose. When you have done the best you can and all you can, you're no less a person if the effort fails. Don't build up a reservoir of hurts, gripes, and bad feelings that can spill over into relationships. Learn to forgive—yourself and others.

*Weighing your options* frees you to do more productive things with your time and energy. Avoid backing yourself into a corner by thinking, "I have no choice." Very few situations hold out only one possible response. For example, you can wash dishes now, later, talk your husband into doing them, or call a friend for a cup of tea and maybe she'll help you do them. Find as many workable answers to problems as possible. Work toward the best one for all concerned, including yourself.

Try to learn new or better ways of relating, communicating, and working with people. Use creative ways to get your point across. Notice how you usually handle anger, anxiety, sadness, joy, excitement, and ambition. How do your responses in these areas come across to others? Look for ways that might get your ideas across in a more effective or nonthreatening way.

Check to see if ministry goals have displaced personal needs. If so, you may have idealized your role as a minister's wife to the point of worshiping it. What about ministry goals and your children? They need to be seen as individuals and not as tokens of their parents' religious zeal. Just as you need not be perfect, neither should your children be pressured to be all-wise and goody-good. Let commitment be an opening rather than a closing of options in your life.

*Building your resources* gives you something to fall back on when the going gets rough. Are you able to face sticky situations without bankrupting your personhood? Three areas are of particular help in coping with stress: physical stamina, intellectual keenness, and spiritual growth.

Stress is first of all a bodily reaction, so your physical well-being is vital. Exercise is one of the best ways of relieving tension, buffering anxiety, and preventing illness. Get involved in some kind of activity that uses the long muscles of your body. Choose an exercise that you can do regularly at least three times a week for about forty-five minutes at a time. Walking is one of the very best exercise habits you can make. Walking is inexpensive, usually handy to do, and flexible as to time and level of performance.

Along with exercise, upgrade your eating habits. Cut out overuse of salt, sugar, caffeine-laden beverages, and fats. Fall in love with fruits and fresh vegetables—your body will thank you for it as long as you live. Have regular physical checkups: prevent rather than cure. A healthy body keeps up a higher resistance level—your first line of defense against stress, depression, and disease.

Mental alertness keeps your mind in a positive mode. A good counter to depression comes from looking outward, finding creative outlets, and renewing your zest in living. Keep up with what's going on in the world. Read, take up a hobby or craft, join a club, enroll in adult education classes, or attend seminars and retreats. Get out of the same old routine for a while to put your life in perspective. Keep in touch with old friends to prevent the loneliness and rootlessness many ministers' wives experience. Build a good support network in your ministry setting. Find persons you can call on for help, professional advice, and companionship.

Find someone who can fill a pastoral role for you. Perhaps a clergyman outside your church parish, a former pastor, a denominational leader, or a teacher can give spiritual direction for you. You might join with another minister's wife or Christian friend to share prayer, Bible study, or ideas about your spiritual pilgrimage. Find ways for your spiritual needs, confessions, or concerns to be expressed. Set aside some private time each day to enjoy solitude. Deepening your faith can come through listening for the quieter assurance of God's care. Look for God's presence in family and friends, the beauty of nature, and the many small things you have to be thankful for each day.

In dealing with persistent stress, seek help before the situation overwhelms you. Your denomination likely provides counseling services that are confidential and at little or no cost. Christian counselors are available who understand both the personal and ministry sides of your life. Find out if your denomination provides funds for ministers' wives to get training in stress management or to attend retreats. Often funds are available if ministers' wives make their needs known.

By all means yield your stress to God. He is not likely to thrust you into a situation that will destroy either your marriage or your commitment to Him. It seems a little simplistic to suggest looking for God's grace in every day, every problem, every person—but He's there. God is realistic in His concern for you: "Every test that you have experienced is the kind that normally comes to people. But God keeps his promise, and he will not allow you to be tested beyond your power to remain firm; at the time you are put to the test, he will give you the strength to endure it, and so provide you with a way out" (1 Cor. 10:13).

## Time Out

What stressors put the most pressure on you now? What change would you like to see take place in these areas? Who can you call on for support as you deal with them?

*Measure your stressors against the very worst thing that could happen in each of the situations. Then hold them up to God:*

Dear Father, Your power stilled the stormy sea and raised the dead. Help me trust this power to calm my inner strife and guide me toward wise choices.

# 6

# Responding to People in the Church

*Joan almost jumped out of her skin when the phone rang. "Dear God, please don't let it be Pam," she pleaded. Pam had become a fixture around the house lately. Neglected by her divorced parents and ignored by those her age, Pam struggled with loneliness. Todd had been right about Pam's needs being too great for one person to meet, yet Joan hated to see her so miserable. Pam's visits and calls, however, soon grew excessive. She wanted more and more attention, approval, and emotional support. Joan dreaded the upset of ending Pam's dependency, yet both of them needed to be set free. "How do I get myself into these things?" Joan wondered. "All I wanted to do was help!"*

So what's the big problem about getting along with people in a ministry field—be nice to them and they'll be nice to you, right? In most cases that's true, but some relationships come up that are not so rosy. Ministers' wives face all types and ages of persons in a typical congregation. These individuals act on all kinds of moods and opinions. Loyalties and social pecking orders affect church fellowships just like any other groups. Since the minister and his family have built-in status in a congregation, they fill a special place in the give-and-take of church relationships.

A minister's wife is not quite staff and not quite layperson. She lacks the clout of elected church leaders or the influence of longtime church members. At times she's a leader, a friend, a target, a counselor, a sore spot, a helper, an intercessor, an unpaid minister, and often a walking bulletin board for information. She will be expected to love everyone but show partiality to no one. She offers church members an outlet for expressing feelings not filled by anyone else.

Many ministers' wives feel a heavy obligation to do well in their husband's congregation, to please everyone. This sense of duty can be rewarding, but it can also be oppressive. One pastor's wife described her fear of displeasing church members like a bad dream, like "a huge gray ball of fuzz that I have to keep pushing all the time so it won't roll backwards and smother me."

Perhaps your relationship to church people is not that overwhelming—good for you! But perhaps you'd like to check out some sticky situations that sometimes come up in church life. If so, read on.

## Congregational Attention

Ever think of yourself as a celebrity? A good many church members may react to you as one. Everyone in the community seems to know who you are within days of coming to the church. You're likely to come in for lots of attention, interest, and curiosity from them. Most of this attention is well intended, growing out of people's goodwill toward their minister's wife.

Celebrity status can be both a plus and a minus. A fine line often separates an enjoyable relationship from a suffocating one. The ministerial "glass house" life-style can become too artificial for normal living. The trick is to tell when the line is being crossed and to pull back from it. Social, emotional, and spiritual support from church members brings much needed encouragement. You'll want to treasure this kind of support as you deal with less pleasant encounters.

Your skill in handling the offbeat, uncomfortable, or frustrating relationships will go a long way toward building role satisfaction for you as a minister's wife. You and those with whom you relate have good days and bad days, grow and change, and sometimes foul up things for everyone. In other words, you and they go through the ordinary difficulties of human experience. The challenge is to relate in effective ways to those who test anyone's patience in the best of times.

### Family Ownership

Sports fans sometimes become very closely identified with their favorite team. Subconsciously the team may come to represent their fantasies or hopes or actually seem an extension of themselves. This close attachment sometimes occurs in relationships between clergy families and congregants.

Some church members may look on the clergy family as extensions of their own religious ideals. They may see the minister and his family as part of their family. This kind of closeness offered to clergy families can be a boon: a sense of welcome and belonging wherever they go in the church community. The blessings of prayer, concern, and practical care generally surround them. Help can be counted on during times of illness, grief, or hardship. Such a loving community frees clergy families from much of the isolation felt by many households in our mobile, self-serving society.

The dark side of this attachment comes when closeness turns into possessiveness. Self-appointed watchers often keep track of the family's activities. They feel free to criticize the family on very personal matters. A minister's son noted, "Everyone tells me what to do, like they were my parents." One minister's wife was both astonished and angered to discover that her small children were grilled each week in Sunday School: "Did you have a babysitter this week? Where did Mommy and Daddy go? Were they with anyone?"

Church members may take a parental attitude toward younger ministers and their wives: "Our sweet little pastor's wife." Such individuals may take it on themselves to advise and instruct: "You ought not to be seen at the city pool in a bathing suit. People will think

you're immodest." They project their own hang-ups onto you, expecting their standards to be obeyed.

Help in dealing with too much attention begins by realizing that it exists. Intrusion into your personal space is not really an attack on you, annoying though it may be. You hold a special place in the lives of these people. Resisting, arguing against, or rejecting your status won't help at all. A certain amount of unwanted attention comes simply as a result of being in a public role. Accept it with good grace.

Before getting all bent out of shape by others' comments, you might want to take a thoughtful look at the image you're creating for the public. A life-style very far out of sync with local custom or accepted Christian values is bound to stir up comment. Some clergy families have been guilty at times of playing a game of psychological hide-and-seek with parishioners by being one thing in public and something else in private. This doesn't mean that you need to give up your privacy or keep every act in plain sight. Rather, check the signals you may be sending out by your words and actions. You may be coming across in ways you don't intend.

Try to help your children understand the special place they share in the lives of church people. Help them deal with too much notice. Suggest some ways they might answer very personal questions, such as: "I'd rather you asked Mom and Dad about that if you don't mind." Encourage them as they face being singled out in public or held up for an example.

Find some helpful ways of responding to pointed comments about personal tastes or behavior. You can be gracious without compromising your worth as a person. You might answer comments by saying: "I certainly haven't thought about it that way." Or, "Your concern is very helpful. I'll keep it in mind." You have no duty to carry out unwelcome suggestions or answer all questions. Responding to them with grace, however, shows not only your openness but also your self-respect. Perhaps these difficult persons test the truth of the gospel in your response so they can really believe it has meaning for themselves.

### Sharing Your Husband

A denominational worker's wife often heard this remark from participants in her husband's seminars: "Thank you for sharing him with us." At first she thought the comment odd for, after all, the seminars were part of his work. But she came to realize that his ministry required a lot of time away from the family in travel, preparation, and meeting with local churches. She was sharing in a very real way by living with an often mentally and physically drained spouse.

You may have reached the conclusion that your mate's *giving* to his ministry results in *taking* from your marriage or family life. That feeling is mutual among wives of helping professionals of all kinds: doctors, counselors, psychologists, law-enforcement officers, firefighters, teachers, and so on. Ministry, however, does seem to have an abundant supply of time grabbers to contend with. Irregular hours and unplanned events seem to be the rule more than the exception.

Then there's the fact you won't be able to share in all of your husband's ministry. Many confidential matters will always be off limits. He will be bound by ministerial ethics in respecting the privacy of those he counsels.

Your husband's contact with persons of the opposite sex may sometimes take on uncomfortable overtones for you. One young minister's wife confessed to anxiety about her husband's relationship with church women. He served as singles minister in a large urban congregation. Many of his clients were attractive, successful career women. His wife, often drained from child care and household chores, felt insecure in her ability to hold her husband's attention or admiration.

Ministry is often very emotionally draining. Your husband may spend a day listening to other people's gripes, heartaches, and problems. He may not appear ready to listen to yours as well. On the other hand, you are not "just another church member" vying for his time.

Ministry events, confidential exchanges, social contacts, and emotional stress are typical ways you share your husband. These and other demands on his time and presence may seem like rivals to your relationship as a couple. They need not drain all your emotional resources, however. These demands can be balanced with practical coping skills.

Work with your husband to see if limits can be set on long hours at the office or endless church meetings. One wife noted, "I got fed up with meetings which start at 7:00 and last until they get tired of talking." A youth minister's wife resented her husband's preoccupation with his youth groups: "Their activities take up all our spare time. I seldom go out alone with Dave—a bunch of kids usually tag along." Excessive demands are really not helpful to either minister or congregants. A reasonable limit can be set on length and number of meetings. You will want to be accessible to those your husband serves, but at the same time you will need to keep some much needed privacy. Being well liked is a powerful motivator for ministers. They are sometimes afraid of limiting their effectiveness by saying no to invitations. They fear hurting someone's feelings by holding back any time at all for personal concerns. These fears may prove valid in a few cases, but failure to keep private time as a couple will prove far more damaging to ministry in the long run.

A typical time grabber for clergy couples is impromptu business talks. Many people take any handy chance to talk with a minister. They prefer not to make office appointments, choosing instead to linger after church services, stand over the table in a restaurant, or hold up shopping at the supermarket. Sometimes these talks are necessary, but just as often they can be handled later. Encourage your husband to steer these casual contacts toward regular office hours or his home visits. People can learn to respect your time as a couple if you respect it also by not giving it away carelessly.

Respect the limits that counseling places on

your husband. Ministry ethics require that matters discussed with a minister be kept in strictest confidence. Don't put pressure on him by asking about counseling sessions. Unless persons involved in counseling wish you to know, don't expect to hear reports on who seeks help and why.

Accept the fact that your husband will come in contact with attractive, interesting women as he serves. His openness, kindness, and concern as a minister may indeed make him vulnerable to some woman's romantic designs—but so can your behavior with male church members. A normal amount of concern is quite necessary. Your husband needs to avoid placing himself in situations that could be misinterpreted. Morbid fear on your part, however, may indicate a deep-seated emotional need.

If you feel uneasy about your husband's attention to church women, you might help clear the air by discussing your feelings with him. Knowing the precautions he takes in private sessions with women, for example, may give you reassurance. Some ministers take their wives along for after-hours sessions. Others make sure a secretary or other church staff person is nearby while sessions take place at the office. Using good common sense in handling contacts with the opposite sex usually takes care of most problems. The best defense against intrusion into your marriage is to keep the relationship growing, interesting, and strong.

Continuing uneasy feelings about your husband's relationship with women, however, may need the help of a reliable counselor to untangle. Your husband may indeed be flattered by the attention or hooked on the "need to be needed" in these relationships. If that's the case, he will want to discover why this is so. You may need to examine your own self-esteem and see how it may be affected by your husband's ministry. You might also wish to strengthen your relationship through marriage enrichment. Ministry might be draining away too much energy, emotional resources, and time from your relationship as a couple. Putting personal and ministry needs in bal-

ance will take a lot of the anxiety out of your relationship.

Ministry is a giving kind of vocation, but giving need not leave your marriage bankrupt. Most congregations realize your need for privacy and don't begrudge you relaxation time. Return their concern by not abusing your privilege as their minister's wife. Sharing your husband's time with others may not always be easy, but it will certainly be necessary in ministry.

### The Other Woman

What about you? How well do you get along with women in your husband's ministry setting? Many ministers' wives express concern about relating to staff wives or women church leaders. A sense of uneasiness often comes in not knowing exactly where you fit in. If you're like most clergy wives, you use a lot of woman's intuition in responding to these relationships. An additional source of help can be found in understanding how any group works. Since you deal with church groups, women's and others, these insights may ease your way in entering them.

Most groups have an informal as well as formal structure. The formal structure may be officers, by-laws, and usual procedures at meetings. The informal structure, however, is more complex and perhaps just as vital as the formal one. Informal group structure has to do with how the group organizes itself: who leads and who follows, who dominates the conversation, who influences decisions, who has power in the group, who sets the pace, and who gives the group cues on behavior. Does all this take place in church women's groups? You bet it does, and the greater your insight into the process the easier you'll find relating to the group.

People who live or work together usually get organized so that things go smoother for everyone. This is true for families, social clubs, churches, and even nations. Over a period of time a pattern of well-defined rules and relationships grows up. This familiar pattern helps people feel comfortable with each other. They rely on each other to act in predictable ways. They come to know each other's strengths and weaknesses and use these factors for the group's benefit.

A newcomer upsets any group's balance. Group members don't know what to make of the newcomer, so they get uneasy. The familiar pattern of relationships has to be adjusted to take the new one in. Everyone's place has to be learned all over again before the group settles into a comfortable pattern. Remember that as a minister's wife, you'll be that newcomer many times. You'll be the focus of adjustment. Some women in the group will actually suffer stress from your presence, and you probably will feel it as well.

Church women will have some expectations about your place among them. As a minister's wife you have a built-in leadership position. Some women may see that role as a threat to their own position. Other women may look forward to new roles for themselves in any changes you might cause. Still others may try to get you as an ally on their side so they might get power in the group. These needs and desires usually are made known in subtle ways: getting close to you, inviting you, avoiding you, quizzing you, and so on. It's simply the group's way of adjusting to the new member.

Keep these points in mind when entering a new group:

• *Group structure.*—Accept the fact that church groups exist. They don't have to be formally organized to have influence on what goes on. Look for these patterns in your ministry setting. They may be based on age, interests, family friendships, economic levels, business ties, or doctrinal concerns. These groups are quite natural and can help people find a comfortable place in the church. The group structure may overlap that of a Sunday School class, mission group, or choir. Or, the structure may take in a wider, informal grouping. You can get some clues from those who cluster together in the halls after services, get together to entertain, or look at one another in making decisions.

• *Group adjustment.*—Just as you go through the process of getting to know people in the church, they are also getting used to you. You

can expect some tension, ambivalence, and hesitation at first. Take it easy on rushing into groups or trying to take charge. Be open to friendships but don't ally yourself too quickly to any one person or viewpoint. For example, one woman might want you to be *her* friend but not friend to another woman who took the opposite side in a past issue. If you can avoid being drawn into one camp, you can likely move smoothly through all groups. Let the various groups see that you're not setting out to be a threat to anyone.

• *Group history.*—Groups take their form because of past happenings. Listen to stories of family ties, early church relationships, or business and political connections. Look for the "sacred cows," those bones of contention between groups. One pastor's wife ran into a "pink vase war" in one move onto a new church field. An elderly woman in the church provided an expensive vase for the communion table flowers. Almost everyone thought the vase inappropriate, if not downright ugly. Yet no one wanted to tackle the job of getting the vase removed. A Sunday School class tried to enlist the pastor's wife for this chore. She happened to know the story behind the vase and the social rivalries involved, and she saved herself a great deal of headache by staying out of the issue. Time and some diplomatic rotation of flower containers eventually solved the problem.

• *Group leaders.*—Group leaders, elected or not, hold the key to decision making. The group checks their reaction before acting. Their quiet yes often speaks louder than a dozen shouted noes. You will not need to abide by everything these leaders say, but you will need to take them into account in building sound relationships. Their views will be helpful in understanding how plans are made and decisions are carried out.

• *Group expectations.*—Try to get some feeling for the group's expectation of you—leader, follower, pacesetter, confidante, one-of-the-gang, inspirational guide, or the like. Decide if you feel comfortable with that role. You might ask some of the leaders what they think would be a good role for you. Their answers may give you clues to expectations held by themselves as well as others in the church.

In entering the group, think about the kind of reception you hope to receive. Is this hope realistic? Does it seem suitable to the current group situation? For example, you may be used to directing the women's mission projects. The new group, however, has its own preferred leader for this task. Can you adjust your hopes to fit into the group structure? Will you be so impatient outside a leadership role that you will be bored or indifferent to the group's work?

There's no guarantee you will be accepted with open arms by any group. You may not even wish to be part of church groups. However, relating to these groups will be part of your life as long as you stay in the church. Learning something about group dynamics can make your life easier. Your sensitivity goes a long way toward gaining people's trust and approval. Since women are in the majority in most churches, your relationship with them gives you a distinct advantage over your husband in understanding what makes the congregation tick.

### Staff Relationships

Serving in a multistaff ministry usually means close, supportive relationships between staff members and their families. Such is not always the case, however. Some clergy couples may be uncomfortable working with other staff or lack skills in relating on any level except a very businesslike one. Some clergy couples fear losing their place in the church power structure when new staff members are hired. Church staff members and their families may never see each other except at church events. Any number of similar situations can make staff relationships strained or, at least, distant.

Concerns expressed by ministers' wives at a retreat give some idea of the kinds of friction that can crop up in staff relationships. Pastors' wives sometimes come across as the "queen bee" or "big mama" of the church. Staff wives then feel they have been either shoved off on the sideline or else are too closely supervised by her. One education minister's wife voiced her resentment at being constantly corrected by the pastor's wife: "She treats me like a child, as though I had no experience in the church at all." Two staff wives in the same church expressed a shared concern: "Our pastor and his wife are so distant. We don't know how to approach them. We don't know whether to include them in our social life or not. We have very little contact except at church." An associate pastor's wife had difficulty deciding how active to be as a leader: "The pastor's wife doesn't seem very interested in being part of church programs. But I don't want to act too forward as though I were better than she or wanted to take her place."

Pastors' wives also had their share of concerns. One wife noted: "Most of the resistance to my husband's leadership is coming from the music minister's wife. She was very close to the former pastor's wife, and I think she resents our coming here very deeply." A young pastor's wife struggled to find her niche in church life: "The education minister and his wife have been here for fifteen years. She really calls the shots. I think she hoped the church would call her husband as pastor."

Another side of staff life was expressed by wives who had to face some rather formidable church secretaries. A youth minister's wife explained: "The pastor's wife is a doll. It's the church secretary who drives me crazy! She decides whose calls go through, even to my own husband. She had her mind made up about me before we moved to town, and it's been war ever since." Another wife noted wistfully, "I wish Miss Emma would retire! She knows everything and everybody, and you'd better be on her good side if you want to get anything done."

These stories reflect some pretty typical potholes in the road to sharing ministry life in a congregation. People act out of their personality. They want to keep up their own popularity or influence in the church. Staff ministers and their wives are not exempt from trying to meet selfish aims in what they do. Fear of dismissal often looms over staff members in their response to pastors and church leaders. Pastors sometimes resent the quick success of new, popular staff ministers after years of struggle in the same areas of work. Ministers who've never shared ministry on a church staff before may not be ready to give up the "one-man-band" role they've always held. These and other issues carry over into social relationships among staff ministers and their families.

If you encounter rough spots in relating to staff members, try to discover what motivates them to act as they do. Some of the same factors that apply to group relationships also play a part here. Anxiety about their influence in the church can be a powerful motive. Self-esteem needs such as the desire for approval can lead to competition. Everyone needs a certain amount of personal space and will defend this turf from others.

Think about how you relate to your husband's ministry colleagues. Do you feel uneasy about their influence over decisions? Do you try to build up support for yourself or your mate at their expense? How do you react to their popularity among church members? If you preceded them in the church, did you help smooth their way into the fellowship? If you are a pastor's wife, do you feel obligated to correct any perceived failings on the part of staff wives? If you are a staff minister's wife, are you able to accept the role the pastor's wife has chosen for herself? If a conflict comes up, have you worked out a way of dealing with the problem? Do you feel free to express your feelings? Can you live with the situation, even if you do not like it?

Find ways of affirming the relationship you share with ministry colleagues and their wives. Accept their need to find a niche in church life. Take advantage of seminars or retreats that deepen skills in team building or give insights into personality dynamics. Get to know colleagues and their wives in settings away from the church. You might be able to offer each a welcome chance to be themselves, to let their hair down in a safe and supportive relationship.

## Choices About Friendships

Friendship with staff colleagues is one thing, but close relationships with church members is another. Being part of a church group such as a Sunday School class allows you to make casual friendships with many people. That kind of friendship is "safe" for a minister's wife. Choosing certain persons from a group as intimate friends may call for tact on your part.

Many ministers' wives choose not to have close friends in their husband's congregation. They fear such relationships will be interpreted as favoritism or trying to run things through a clique. Most church members don't object to their minister or his wife having close friends. Some church members, however, do take exception to the idea. Past unpleasant experiences in the church probably are the reason for any objection. You will need to weigh the possible effects before making a decision about your present situation.

Take into account your need for close relationships. See if that need can be met within the church's expectations. One minister's wife recalled being told quite bluntly by a pulpit committee not to make special friends in the church. She endured this demand in an isolated rural community about two years. She finally discreetly reached out to several women her age in the church. No problem resulted, but she was never able to feel quite free in the relationship.

Another point to consider is that of confidentiality. It is always wise to consider carefully how much personal information you share and with whom. You will want to test relationships before speaking too freely or investing too much of yourself, church members or not. One wife's experience in a rather trivial incident points up the need for caution. She casually mentioned her husband's choice of sleepwear while talking with a close church friend. She was astonished to discover that by the next evening's midweek service, her husband's silk pajamas had become the main topic of conversation all over town. While this incident resulted only in some good-natured kidding, the potential for harm in other matters is quite plain.

If you choose not to make close friendships within the congregation, other options are possible. Wives of helping professionals such as doctors, lawyers, counselors, and psychologists share some of the same disruptions of their home life as you have with a minister husband. You may find friends among ministers' wives or members of other denominations. Inquire if a local ministers' wives group exists. If not, perhaps you might contact these wives to form a support group.

Cultivate sound friendships wherever you find them. One minister's wife recalled, "One of my best friends didn't go to any church. She was one of the few people who allowed me to be myself. It was nice not to play 'preacher's wife' all the time." You need not starve yourself of companionship because of church attitudes or situations. However, don't allow any friendship to hinder *being* a friend to church acquaintances. Sharing fellowship with persons of all ages and backgrounds can be a very enriching process in your life. All persons, even the difficult ones, reveal the infinite variety of human experience. They can open your eyes to the great human need for love, respect, acceptance, and Christian grace.

### Trying to Be Something to Everybody

A good many ministers' wives see themselves as little more than public relations persons. One pastor's wife put it this way: "My husband is always saying things like: 'Speak to Mrs. So-and-so. Compliment Mrs. Whoever on her flower arrangement. If you see last Sunday's visitors in town, make sure they know who you are and invite them back.' On and on, day after day. I feel like a politician's wife."

And she's right! A lot of your time and energy will go into building good relationships if you share any part of your husband's ministry

at all. But that kind of activity draws people into a more loving, caring, attentive circle. Isn't that a valid part of life, let alone ministry?

The apostle Paul seemed to think so: "By our purity, knowledge, patience, and kindness we have shown ourselves to be God's servants—by the Holy Spirit, by our true love" (2 Cor. 6:6). These traits help you to relate to all kinds of people in all kinds of circumstances. This openhearted outlook on people not only spreads kindness but also accepts unkindness without getting even. Gentleness and sweetness of spirit don't mean you're a pushover for others' bad temper, but rather that you're a mature person who can handle inadequacies in others. Most of all, that kind of spirit shows that you've come to grips with your own faults in a redemptive, healing way.

Ministers' wives don't learn this kind of response in a charm school; it is God-given. Genuine love and concern for others grow out of fellowship with God through the Holy Spirit. Let this kind of love shine through, and all relationships will take on new meaning. Only love awakens love in others.

### Time Out

What person causes you the greatest difficulty in relating?

Which of his or her personality traits do I most fear in myself? Is my response a reflection of this fear?

*Review your difficult relationships, as though you could start all over again. Think of the changes you'd like to see take place. Then share them with God:*

Dear Father, You have the power to make all things new. Forgive me when I forget this possibility with those who cause me pain. Help us come together in Your bond of peace and love.

# 7

# Facing the Rough Spots

*Joan answered the door and was surprised to see Ruth. Ruth's husband had been transferred, and her family was moving today. "I just couldn't leave without telling you how much you've meant to me these past few months," Ruth began, tears filling her eyes. "I didn't think I could make it after we lost Jimmy. Just knowing I could talk to you has helped so much." She hugged Joan and ran back to the car.*

*Joan recalled that awful day when Ruth's teenage son killed himself. Todd asked her to stay with Ruth until funeral arrangements were completed. Joan dreaded that request, for she never knew what to say to grieving people. She felt so helpless just sitting and listening as Ruth poured out her anguish that long afternoon. And then the phone calls, lingering moments of Ruth's sorrow and guilt over her son's death. Through it all Joan had doubted her usefulness in helping Ruth. Now she thought, "Maybe I helped after all."*

Ministers' wives usually face a lot of crisis times. They deal with loss in their own lives as well as go through it with family, friends, and ministry contacts. Loss is a common experience, not only in death but also in terminal illness, disability, loss of job, divorce, broken relationships, and failed dreams. These times of loss can stir up a wide range of feelings. Typical responses may include shock, anger, denial, guilt, and despair.

You can cope with your own grief and help others by understanding some of the physical, emotional, and spiritual effects of loss. Every person's grief experience is unique, but some common factors are shared during crisis times. This chapter will look at some of these general factors and also suggest ways of responding to them.

## Working Through Loss and Grief

Any deep sense of loss—job termination, divorce, death, separation, serious illness, radical life-style change—triggers grief. Grief is a way of showing that we've been hurt. Our sense of security has been badly shaken. We feel attacked at a deep inner level. As a result, many powerful feelings well up. We realize that all is not well, and we fear that things can never be right again. Working through grief and loss means dealing with these feelings in a meaningful way.

Accepting and expressing real grief begins a healing process. Grieving helps get over the shock of loss. Expressing grief is both natural and helpful. Feelings can be released in ways that free us from the grip of lasting despair.

### Feelings Involved in Loss

Individuals react to loss in different ways. Some persons are very open and vocal about their feelings. Others, however, may show little outward sign of emotion. Most people do react inwardly to grief in similar ways. Pinpointing the degree of emotion a person feels may not always be easy. Feelings may come quickly and all at once, or may come gradually over a period of time. One person may go through all kinds of emotional upheaval connected with a loss, while another may experience only a little. Some understanding of the feelings usually involved in grief will be helpful in spotting a person's reaction.

Typical feelings connected with loss are disbelief, anxiety, guilt, anger, and despair. Persons often move through these stages in dealing with their loss. However, these feelings do not always come in any set order, and some may not come at all. These feelings, however, are usually present to some degree.

• *Disbelief.*—This feeling works as an emotional cushion to help deal with loss. Numbness may follow the initial shock. The more sudden or unexpected the loss, the greater disbelief may be. Even after a long illness or anticipated crisis, the actual moment of loss can still be traumatic. Typical reactions of disbelief: How can this be? Some mistake has been made. This is not possible. This can't be happening to me. This is just a bad dream that will go away.

• *Anxiety.*—Realizing the extent of loss often creates anxiety. Panic arises over what may happen or what to do next. Helpless feelings may take over. Typical anxiety reactions: How can I face this? What will become of me? Where will I go? What will I do? Who can I depend on now?

• *Guilt.*—Loss makes us want to find an explanation, place blame, or identify someone responsible for the situation. Our own failings come into sharp focus. Memories of hasty decisions, unwise moves, or indifference often crop up. Common guilt reactions: Why didn't I see this coming? If only I had acted in time. I should have known this would happen. I should have done something.

• *Anger.*—Loss upsets our sense of well-being. We feel very threatened. Anger is a natural reaction to such feelings. But anger can be one of the hardest feelings to handle in the grief process. It is both hard to hear and to express, especially at a death. Other feelings seem more appropriate, so we tend to deny any anger. Any kind of loss, however, can create awareness of betrayal, unfairness, or abandonment. The anger may focus on self, on others involved in the loss, or on God for allowing the loss to happen.

Anger often gets denied or disguised as another kind of feeling. This approach can turn anger inward upon self. Denied or suppressed anger causes guilt. Increased guilt in turn makes more anger. A vicious cycle of anger/denial/guilt/anger can take hold, often trapping the grieving person in despair.

Anger at loss can be helpful. This emotion may be a way of declaring selfhood. Anger can show the desire to overcome a bad situation, to strike back at pain. Typical anger responses: Why did this happen to me? God doesn't care or this wouldn't have happened. Why did he [she, they] treat me this way? I could just kill him [her, them]! He [she, they] did this just to hurt me. I'll show him [her, them]!

• *Despair.*—At some point the reality of loss begins to sink in. Fears about other possible losses—health, business, family members, own life—may crowd into the present grief. Loss of hope may block any thought of going on with daily routines. Wanting to give up or die sometimes seems the best way out. Typical despair responses: Life just isn't worth living any more. I don't think I can go on without him [her, the job, or whatever was lost]. I'd rather be dead than live this way.

Acknowledging and expressing grief feelings helps put the loss into human terms we can deal with. Grieving often gives a sense of balance and hope for the future. The loss can be seen as a part of normal life experiences, that we are not the only one to go through a loss. Such discoveries are vital in recovering from loss, as well as rebuilding self-esteem.

### Healthy Grieving

The shock of loss dumps an emotional load on us. Grief helps lighten the load when done in a healthy way. Four basic steps can help in the grief process:

*1. Own the loss.*—Loss has occurred and can't be wiped away. Accepting this simple fact reaffirms self while seeing the loss in real terms as change.

*2. Own your feelings.*—Anger, guilt, despair—whatever the feelings may be—show your inner reaction to the loss. To have such feelings is not sinful. Jesus responded to Lazarus' death by grieving. He acknowledged His grief and spoke to the grief of Martha, Mary, and other friends (John 11:17-38). Jesus expressed His grief openly with tears. On this occasion and others, He felt and showed a wide range of emotions. Jesus gave us an example of healthy response to feelings. He

**BARRIERS TO HEALTHY GRIEF**

helped those around Him deal with their needs in a redemptive way.

Try to pick up on the feelings that go along with a loss. Accept these feelings as a normal reaction to loss: "I feel bad about this. Things are going to be different now. How will I ever find strength to face it all?" This kind of insight helps view loss in terms of change. Ways can be found to make change more bearable, to make sense out of it. This kind of grieving does not block or delay recovery, yet the reality of loss is accepted and faced.

*3. Reach out for help.*—Concern and care from others offer a way of dealing with the change brought by loss. Help with immediate needs shows that life is indeed possible and can be worth living. Family and friends cannot remove the loss, but they can lend support in facing it. The pain of isolation or loneliness can be eased.

*4. Deal with spiritual concerns.*—Loss often brings all of life into sharp focus. Aims and priorities stand out in contrast to the effect of a crisis. In fact, *crisis* means a turning point or time of decision. Feelings about God, life purpose, and faith take on meaning as in perhaps few other situations. Worship, prayer, Bible reading, and commitment can offer a special kind of relief during times of deep loss.

Grief and loss often force persons to exam-

ine their priorities, the concerns that absorb most of their energy and resources. Sorting out feelings can lead to spiritual awareness and growth. The apostle Paul noted the spiritual maturity that loss can bring: "trouble produces endurance, endurance brings God's approval, and his approval creates hope. This hope does not disappoint us, for God has poured out his love into our hearts by means of the Holy Spirit, who is God's gift to us" (Rom. 5:3-5).

Awareness of loss, feelings, need for help, and spiritual concerns are helpful parts of grieving. Allow them to guide your own approach to grief and your understanding of others' needs as they face times of loss.

**Helping Others Deal with Loss**

Doubts about personal skill need not prevent you from offering comfort to others. You may fear not saying or doing the right thing, or not being able to help at all. These concerns are valid, but even professional counselors face them too. Spontaneous feelings of empathy drawn from your own experience can be good clues in helping others. Some general but useful items to remember about helping:

*1. Be there.*—Your presence shows concern and support. Express your feelings in simple, sincere terms. Offer help in practical ways such as washing dishes, caring for a small child, running errands, and the like. Maybe the most needed thing you could do is simply sit with the person for a while.

2. *Listen.*—Grieving persons often need a sympathetic ear to hear their feelings. They don't want their loss denied or sugarcoated with false hopes or belittled by pious talk. When the person wishes to talk, show an accepting attitude. Let him or her give free rein to expressing feelings. However, if the person doesn't wish to share feelings, don't prod. The point is to let the person talk out what he or she is going through.

3. *Be supportive.*—If intense or negative feelings come out, don't reject or deny them. All you need to do at this point is simply acknowledge the feelings. You might say: "I can see that this situation is really making you hurt [angry, upset, sad, or whatever the feeling seems to be]." Let the grieving person take it from there without correction or explanation from you.

4. *Go slow on advice.*—Grieving persons often beg: "Tell me what to do." You will find it tempting to take charge. However, the grieving person needs to make his or her own decisions to the greatest degree possible. Find out what needs to be done and simply list the options. Let the person choose what to do. Loss makes persons very vulnerable to pressure. Avoid pushing your own ideas. You really won't want to be responsible for leading them into something against their will.

5. *Encourage positive actions.*—Offer to help the person carry out decisions. Give moral support, but don't try to do everything for the person. Making decisions and acting on them can be comforting and healing during recovery from loss.

6. *Keep in contact.*—As time goes on, give some sign of continuing concern. You aren't responsible for reorganizing the person's life after a loss. After showing an appropriate amount of concern, pull back a while. You can be encouraging without being overly meddlesome.

If you sense the grieving person has deep-seated emotional problems, don't hesitate to suggest a counselor. Know your own limitations in helping. One of the wisest things in helping is to know when to refer. You might say: "Have you thought of talking with . . . ?" Let the person explore the idea without forcing the issue. You might offer help in finding a professional counselor or in getting information. The grieving person, however, needs to decide about seeking help on his or her own.

These basics in the grief process indicate some things you can do in helping others. If you are not trained in crisis intervention, don't feel bad about your limits. Being a minister's wife doesn't imply tackling everyone's problems. Grieving persons respond to heartfelt words and show of concern. You can find these helps in your own experience.

Let's turn to some other issues ministers' wives find hard to handle: negative criticism, anger and conflict, and ministry crises.

## Handling Negative Criticism

Criticism, no matter how gently stated or well-intended, seems to make most of us a little nervous. Negative remarks about self reach deeply into our sense of worth and esteem. Dealing with criticism, therefore, can help us feel good about ourselves as well as keep relationships on a more comfortable level.

Criticism can be useful in working out differences of opinion or clearing up problems. However, a lot of criticism does not settle anything. This negative kind of criticizing often comes in the form of put-downs or petty nit-picking. Such criticism can be a way of building up the critic's ego at someone else's expense.

You have every right to reject unfair criticism. Put-downs are tokens of insensitivity and rudeness. You can do yourself a favor by resisting the harmful effects of such remarks. Any kind of criticism, fair or not, can hurt if you let it.

A big part of handling negative criticism has to do with motive. What does the critic mean by his or her words? Does the critic want to hurt you or simply lack the skill to express ideas in a better way? The critic might actually be sincere, have a justified complaint, and want to be helpful. That kind of criticism comes from a good motive. You will want to respond by looking honestly at the problem and working through it. Persons can use criticism, however, in misguided ways: to express anger, to force behavior change, or to belittle. That kind of critic has a poor motive and is likely dumping personal shortcomings on you. You can respond to that kind of criticism without becoming defensive, though doing so takes some effort and concern on your part.

Accepting criticism for what it's worth can take some of the sting out of it. If the critic has a poor motive, your calm response shows that you will not be put down or manipulated. Handling negative criticism skillfully can free you from emotional pain. Consider these steps in answering critics:

1. *Hear the critic out.*—Listen to reasons or explanations for the critic's feelings. You might be able to pick up on motive and see if the criticism holds any truth.

2. *Test the truth of criticism.*—How much of the criticism is valid complaint and how much is anger or anxiety? If you don't hear of any actual wrongdoing on your part, forget the remarks. Do hold open the possibility that you came across in a way not intended, or that you were misunderstood.

3. *Resist striking back.*—No matter how good you think it might feel, don't let your feelings run away with you. Neither sincere nor insincere critics will be helped by an outburst from you. Say something neutral: "I hadn't thought about it that way. Tell me more of how you feel." Or: "I can see that you are concerned about this." A calm response will encourage sincere critics to get at the heart of their complaint with less tension. Insincere critics may realize you aren't buying their line and back off. At least, you may have avoided an argument.

4. *Don't let unjust criticism sink in.*—Take remarks with a grain of salt. Don't expect to please everyone all the time. You can't control what people say, but you can control how you react to their words.

5. *Affirm your worth as a person.*—If you're not at fault, inwardly tell yourself so: "I'm sorry to hear this, but I'm not responsible for this unfair criticism." Even if you make a mistake, you are no less a person for it. Acknowledge your error when due: "You're right. That wasn't the best thing to do." Owning faults in a gracious way shows that you think well of yourself and act responsibly.

Try to take a balanced view of criticism. All persons will not respond to you as you'd like. Others will interpret your actions in light of their own experience. Their personality, background, and expectations will color their opinions. Accept these different views without being hurt by them. Others' remarks often tell more about them as persons than about you.

### Dealing with Anger and Conflict

Anger and conflict are perhaps among the hardest things to face in human relationships. Yet these happenings are both natural and inevitable when people live and work together. Folks are bound to disagree. Handling anger or conflict in healthy ways can result in numerous blessings. People can channel feelings in ways that deal with problems and at the same time keep harmony in the relationship. In fact, conflict can lead to creative approaches to issues when worked through in a positive way.

Anger sets the stage for conflict. A main barrier in dealing with anger is that feelings tend to be denied or ignored until a major conflict is well under way. Such drastic clashes are not really necessary. Understanding what takes place in conflict can make it less awesome and dreaded. Let's look first at some elements involved in anger.

#### Understanding Anger

Anger may be the least understood of all feelings. People fear having anything to do with an angry person. They also fear losing control of their own anger. Because of these and other fears associated with anger, this feeling is often condemned as sinful. Christians are sometimes led to believe that anger should be denied or prevented at all costs. Yet anger at threat, injustice, or wrongdoing is not only natural but appropriate.

Anger, like other feelings, is part of a normal

emotional response. The Bible speaks of God's anger (Ps. 30:5; Jer. 3:12). Jesus expressed anger as a result of His concern about human conditions (Mark 3:5; 11:15). He used His anger in such a way as to mend injustices and correct untruths. Jesus focused His anger on issues. He did not use anger to destroy persons or break relationships. The Bible clearly identifies this wholesome way of handling anger: "If you become angry, do not let your anger lead you into sin, and do not stay angry all day" (Eph. 4:26). This kind of control grows out of maturity, care, and integrity in wisely expressing anger.

Anger tends to be suppressed in group settings. People may feel embarrassed at strong emotion. They assume that if anger can be ignored, it will go away. However, nothing could be further from reality. Ignoring others' anger merely lets feelings build up under the surface. Then some minor issue may come up which triggers an outburst of anger all at once. The issue is often far less important than the intense feelings might imply.

Anger can also be mishandled by calling it something else. Some people may not realize their own anger because they've denied it so long. They may have learned to cover anger as depression, anxiety, or guilt. Not all depression, anxiety, or guilt grows out of suppressed

anger, to be sure. But if such feelings remain unexplained, anger may be at their root.

People sometimes disguise their anger in subtle forms: gossip, criticism, casting suspicion on others, or manipulating people through underhanded means. An inwardly angry person may haggle over every detail or continually be upset over small things. Anger, in fact, may take a variety of forms and a wide range of intensity in expression.

You likely react to others' anger in much the same way you face it in yourself. If you acknowledge and deal with your anger in a healthy way, you will be less troubled by the feeling in others. If you deny or suppress anger, then you will likely want others to treat their anger in the same way. You won't feel very comfortable when others try to express anger toward you or in your presence.

Dealing with others' anger begins with awareness of feelings. Let the angry person know you are aware of his or her intense feeling: "I may be mistaken, but I have the feeling you are upset about something. You don't have to tell me, but I wanted you to know I'm concerned." This kind of statement allows the angry one to feel understood. You need not try to justify or resolve the person's anger, simply show your awareness of the situation. You've allowed the angry person to focus on the feel-

**TYPES OF ANGER RESPONSE**

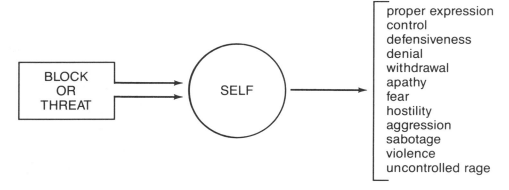

proper expression
control
defensiveness
denial
withdrawal
apathy
fear
hostility
aggression
sabotage
violence
uncontrolled rage

ing. This response may help clarify the issue that provoked the anger.

Other steps in dealing with anger may involve confrontation, statement of concern, forgiveness, and reconciliation. Anger is sometimes a sign of genuine care. Someone totally indifferent to problems will seldom bother to get worked up over them. You might suggest that the angry one share his or her feelings with a trusted church leader (pastor, deacon, or elder, for example). This leader might serve as a go-between in opening up discussion with the parties involved. Such discussion may clear up errors, misunderstanding, or strained relationships.

Your calm, open response to anger helps create a setting in which angry ones feel free to deal with their feelings. You can help them express anger in a helpful way. Coping with anger in a church setting really requires cooperation from the whole fellowship. Everyone needs to join in creating an atmosphere of respect and sensitivity toward feelings. You can help model that kind of attitude.

### Understanding Conflict

Conflict generally comes when more than one option is available in deciding an issue. People have differing methods, goals, or principles in mind. Agreeing on an answer may bring all these differences into contact. Conflict is often the result. Conflict, then, need not be an undesirable situation. Conflict can be good if it opens up more options and if people are free to choose the best course among them.

Conflict, of course, can have very negative effects. Personal hurt, withdrawal from the group, and division can result when conflict gets out of hand. In the midst of conflict, persons may lose sight of the issue and resort to name-calling or personality clashes. Group members may be forced to take sides in protecting their point of view. Group members then become frustrated in dealing with one another.

Attitudes about anger and conflict, past experience, or lack of skill in expressing concerns may block a healthy conflict process. In addition, parties to the conflict may not state the real reason for their anger. For example, conflict may come up over hiring the church's first minister of music. Disagreement may *outwardly* focus on salary, job description, or such details. *Inwardly* the real issue may center on the Jones family's control over the music program: Mr. Jones has served for years as a lay music director, Mrs. Jones plays the organ, and so forth. This kind of hidden agenda of dislikes, resentments, and fears may be at work in provoking the conflict. These hidden issues may stew for a long time before the subject ever comes to a public discussion or vote.

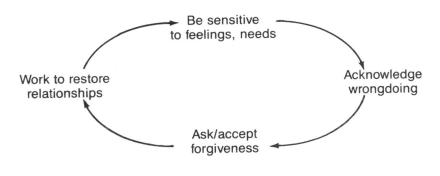

**FORGIVENESS CYCLE**

You will face conflict in your family or another personal arena. Cope with your concern by taking a new look at the conflict process. First, accept the idea that *conflict is not bad and need not be destructive*. Encourage this attitude in all parties to the dispute. Conflict as a process of change and growth can be understood and worked through if everyone is willing to try.

Second, *spot conflicts in the making*. Common signs of growing conflict: foot-dragging about decisions, avoiding the issue at hand, refusing to voice an opinion, anxiety in talking about the issue, or strained relationships. Try to get feelings and needs in focus at this point. Deal with concerns rather than personalities so that the real problem can be identified.

Third, *look for areas of agreement*. See if a common goal unites all sides to the dispute. If so, focus on that goal. For example, the whole family may agree that the den needs redecorating but differ on colors, decor, or amount to be spent. List all the possibilities in settling the issue. Help the parties weigh the options to find the best solution for everyone. Allow enough time for feelings to settle and agreement to build before pushing for a final decision.

Finally, *help all parties feel good about themselves* whatever the decision may be. All kinds of feelings emerge during conflict. Some will see themselves as winners, while others feel like losers. Some individuals may have a hard time accepting the decision, some may gloat at success, while others may feel anxiety over the upset. Look for a way to celebrate the decision that affirms each person's part in ending the conflict. Thank each one for sharing information, cooperating, or helping find a workable answer. Express hope that all have grown in love through their shared efforts in working through the problem.

Each success in working through a conflict makes the process easier the next time. Even if a solution can't be found, the wholesome response to conflict builds trust and lessens the threat of future disagreements. This fact applies to marriage, family life, and other relationships in which conflict arises.

Most people react to conflict with a great deal of stress. Typically levelheaded people may say or do unfortunate things while under pressure. Some of this outburst may be aimed at you. Try to resist judging or rejecting the person. He or she likely struggled with feelings until an outburst seemed the only way to get the point across. You need not condone such outbursts, but you will want to take them in stride. Assure the person that he or she can get a fair hearing without using such tactics. State your awareness of his or her feelings.

Working through conflict is a ministry of reconciliation—God's grace is being lived out in a practical way. Once persons realize they need not be destroyed in working through conflict, they can experience real growth. Trust can replace aggression, name-calling, unfair tactics, and rage in settling disagreements. Everyone's personhood can be affirmed and God's purpose fulfilled: "Happy are those who work for peace; God will call them his children!" (Matt. 5:9).

### Facing Ministry Crises

An unhappy trend toward forced termination, pressure on ministry performance, and rapid staff turnover seems to describe much of modern church life. Ministers and their families face a lot of uncertainty in these times. Ministers' wives can be deeply affected by ministry upheavals in both personal and family relationships. You will want to look at the impact of such an event in your own experience and find some support should it occur.

You can soften the blow of ministry crises by taking stock of them now, before they take place. Think of the worst thing that could happen in your present ministry situation: forced resignation, sudden crippling illness, or some similar outcome you dread. With that event in mind, think about what you could do to cope. This process is a psychological aid in facing the shock. Looking at the worst possible outcome helps you work backward from that point so you can find steps in dealing with the crisis.

If you are now facing a crisis, begin some steps that can ease the situation. First, look for ways to buy time in dealing with the problem. Avoid rushing into decisions if at all possible.

Encourage your husband as he negotiates with church leaders for adequate time to settle your affairs and find another position. Find out how much income is needed to meet basic necessities for about a three-month period. See if the church would be willing to cover that expense or more in a severance package. If all else fails, think about how you might handle financial needs: savings, personal loans, denominational aid, and the like. If you feel that your finances are not as well managed as they might be, begin working toward a solid financial cushion. Improving your financial resources takes a lot of anxiety out of any kind of emergency situation.

List persons you could turn to for support or assistance during crisis times: family, friends, denominational leaders, fellow ministers, or community helping professionals. Think of practical ways these persons could help you. To whom could you go to share your feelings of loss, grief, or anger at this time? What workshops, seminars, or retreats offer help in dealing with ministry crises that you might attend? Do you know how to go about getting help from denominational agencies in case of forced termination?

Help your children understand what happens in ministry crises. Small children often become frightened by the anxiety they sense in adults around them. They may blame themselves for the problem, and they imagine all sorts of horrible things happening to the family. Teens sometimes become bitter toward God or the church if they sense injustice in the situation. They can easily feel alienated from ministry as a result of real or perceived mistreatment at the hands of church members. One minister's child was told by a playmate: "My daddy hates your daddy, and he's going to run your daddy out of town." That kind of encounter needs some realistic explanation from you, plus some reassurance about the family's role in ministry.

Reach into your spiritual resources for help in facing crises. God does not love you any less for having to face the rough spots of serving Him. Even if mistakes were made, you and your family still have worth and potential in God's sight. Go deeper into your understanding of ministry. Just what does it mean to share your life with one who serves a local church, goes on the mission field, or leads a denominational agency? Have you overrated the ideals of ministry in judging your situation? Have you underrated the small victories that faithful service brings?

The apostle Paul cannot be accused of having it easy as a minister of the gospel, yet he could find the grace to say: "God in his mercy has given us this work to do, and so we do not become discouraged. We put aside all secret and shameful deeds; we do not act with deceit, nor do we falsify the word of God. In the full light of truth we live in God's sight and try to commend ourselves to everyone's good conscience. We are often troubled, but not crushed; sometimes in doubt, but never in despair; there are many enemies, but we are never without a friend; and though badly hurt at times, we are not destroyed. At all times we carry in our mortal bodies the death of Jesus, so that his life also may be seen in our bodies" (2 Cor. 4:1-2,8-10).

### Time Out

What part of sharing a life in ministry is roughest for you?

How have you been able to cope with rough times in the past?

How can the strengths and skills you found then help you now?

*Take a fresh look at your concerns, as though they belonged to someone else. Speak the words of concern and hope to yourself that you would say to another struggler. Then share them with God:*

Dear Father, You promised not to test me more than I can bear. Help me feel Your guiding Spirit so that I can face the rough times with courage, wisdom, and endurance for Your kingdom's sake.

# 8

# Making It Over the Long Haul

*Joan glanced in the mirror once more before leaving for the church with Todd. They were being honored with a reception on their wedding anniversary. "Can it be possible," Joan asked herself, "I've been married to a minister for fifteen years?" A lot had happened in those years: six moves, five churches, four children, three cars, two dogs, and one tornado. But she had survived them all more or less with a growing sense of wonder. She had changed too. Gone was that awkward, hesitant young woman who could barely face a church women's group. Now she could face them and sometimes even amaze them with her grasp of the situation. But there was still a long way to go. Todd dreamed of taking a graduate degree, perhaps teaching. Joan began some thought about finishing her own college education, about becoming a social worker. God had so much more to show her about servanthood in reaching out to people. "Yes," she decided, "I've just started to get my act together. The best is yet to be."*

Why change? Why do people feel compelled to improve themselves or their world? Perhaps because they sense things could be better, life could be fuller, and the jumble of events around them could have meaning. Philosophers sometimes see this yearning as the shadow of Eden lingering in human experience. Certainly our inner being, made in the image of God, hungers for more than mere survival. Christian faith calls for growth, maturity, and depth in spiritual wisdom.

Recent trends in self-actualization stirred many people to take a new look at themselves, their sex roles, and their relationships. People are asking a lot of questions about their day-to-day needs and how these needs can be met. Often this process has given off more heat than light, confusing the issues as often as clearing

them. In the long run, each person faces the same age-old questions: "Who am I? What is my reason for being, and how am I to take my place in the world in which I find myself?" Dealing realistically with these questions opens the way to your potential. The future can take on direction and purpose rather than aimlessness.

Facing the future means accepting the reality of change. We age, our environment alters, inventions shake our understanding of the world, natural calamities remind us of our frailty, and social trends leave us guessing. Change, however, can be used to our advantage. We have it in our power to bring about change when needed. We have God's grace to face change's effects.

## Growing as a Person

You and everything around you are in the process of change. Sameness in life may only show that change is gradual and not very dramatic. In time, however, change does become visible, and you may be shocked by the impact. Try glancing through an old school yearbook, looking at your wedding pictures, or going back to a former home. Change really has been taking place all along. Personal growth is a way of working through and building on the forces of change already at work in your life.

Change sometimes comes in a very dramatic way through crises. Life may seem to jerk along from one of these peak moments to the next without much rhyme or reason. Or, sudden success can lift you to a whole new realm of activity. Have you noticed how some persons collapse under the weight of success? Politicians, entertainment personalities, and sports figures give ample evidence of struggles with fame and fortune. Growing as a person can help put dramatic change in balance.

For the Christian, growth is both a personal and a spiritual quest. The New Testament challenges each believer to "come together to that oneness in our faith and in our knowledge of the Son of God; we shall become mature people, reaching to the very height of Christ's full stature. . . . by speaking the truth in a spirit of love, we must grow up in every way to Christ, who is the head" (Eph. 4:13,15). These spiritual aims can't begin to take hold without positive and active growth in ourselves as persons.

At a more down-to-earth level, you'll want to make the most of all the events life brings your way: the new baby, the job, the insights, the changing scene. Growing helps you cope in a practical way, using the gifts and abilities you have. Choosing to grow gives you more control over what happens in your life. Intentional growth works because its process is realistic:

• *The aim of growth is not human perfection.*—You'll still make mistakes, feel limitations, and have needs no matter how much you grow. That's not the point. Growth, instead, helps you be yourself, be more of who and what God created you to be. Power for this kind of growth comes from God's grace.

• *The focus of growth is not on changing your real self.*—You were born with a unique set of traits. Growth cannot and need not change these givens. Any growth guide that promises to overlook or alter these traits will only lead to failure and frustration. Redemption means that the real you is worth saving.

• *The pattern for growth is not based on someone else's personality.*—Others may inspire or provide helpful insights, but they cannot decide your inner direction or fit their own accomplishments to your need. Book stores are full of marvelous accounts of rich and famous persons offering their example as your guide. But you probably don't have a maid to do your work or a secretary or a lot of money to burn while copying their style. Look for meaning in your own life, not theirs.

• *The purpose of growth is not to force your individuality on others.*—Current self-actualization ideals often stress a "me first" attitude—do your own thing regardless of husband, children, employer, friends, moral values, or social responsibility. This attitude shows up in abrasive conduct, strained relationships, and just plain bad manners. Self-glory covers up personal need without dealing with it. Growth means dealing with the reality of self in relation to others, so that their needs can get met also.

Intentional, redemptive growth builds on

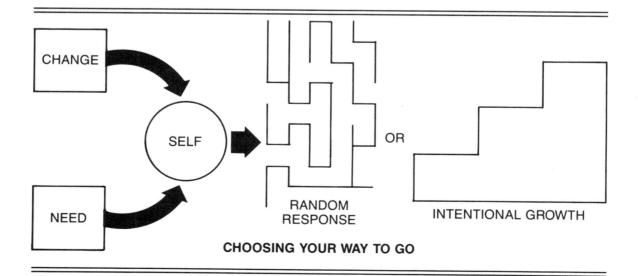

**CHOOSING YOUR WAY TO GO**

who you are by taking into account both assets and liabilities, strengths and weaknesses. Learning your identity as a person gives you an idea of what you can do and where you can go with your life. Few people come close to reaching their potential. There's always room to expand and enhance your abilities, gifts, and wisdom. Every time you take a new growth step, the next one seems easier and more possible to achieve.

God's grace through the Holy Spirit provides the strength and insight for self-understanding. Personal weakness or limitation need not be a barrier to learning His purpose. Of more importance is your willingness to take risks in reaching for God's purpose in your life. When you're ready to take an honest, realistic, redemptive look at yourself, He's ready to help you grow into the wonderful person you can be.

### Locating Growth Needs

Growth begins at a point of need. Readiness for growth, in fact, often shows up as a sense of "dis-ease" in some area of your life. Concern, tension, restlessness, or discomfort may mean that you're unhappy with the way things are and that you're ready to move on to a new level. Change often stirs up this sense of need.

You can block growth at this point by denying your feelings. You can let fear, pride, self-blame, or inaction get in the way of making the situation better. You can suppress growth needs but not do away with them. You can also let past mistakes or failures hold you back. Understanding and accepting mistakes and failures can help you avoid them in the future.

Look at the following areas in your life. Do you sense areas in which you'd like to see change or improvement?

- Self-awareness
- Physical appearance, health
- Emotional outlook
- Recreation, hobbies
- Marriage relationship
- Parenting skills
- Career or talents
- Intellectual powers
- Communication skills
- Decision making
- Support system
- Stress management
- Devotional life
- Spiritual gifts

You may not find growth concerns in all areas, but do check any need for attention. Select one area you feel you'd like to do something about. Keep this concern in mind while reading about the growth process.

### Choosing Growth Goals

Once you've located an area in which you'd like to see improvement or change, the first step calls for deciding some goals that bring the desired result. For example, suppose you choose the area of decision making as a growth point. What specific part of decision making troubles you—setting priorities, getting facts in order, deciding between options, foreseeing the probable effects of decisions, fear of failure or mistakes? Try to get a clear focus on what hinders decision making for you.

Zeroing in on the cause of your concern helps you take the second step: deciding what

---

This is where I am now
(area of growth need):

This is where I want
to go (growth goal):

℞

_____    _____

_____    _____

change you'd like to see take place in the situation. What needs to take place to make things go better or end the problem? For example, suppose you'd like to set priorities better. Look at how you set priorities now and compare that with how you'd like to set them. The difference is your growth goal. You might say: "I don't set priorities at all. I just tend to deal with whatever makes the greatest demand on me at the time. What I'd like to do is plan my day so I could have some free time, so I wouldn't leave necessary things undone or put things off until they overwhelm me." Planning priorities for using time would be your growth goal in this case.

Finally, decide on ways to measure whether growth goals are realistic, whether plans are working, and whether the change taking place is what you want. How will you know when your growth goal has been reached? Measuring your progress is an important part of growth. It helps keep you on track and gives a sense of accomplishment. That's why goals need to be very specific: "I will give each day's activities a priority rank so that I do the necessary things first." Stating the goal clearly helps so much more than saying, "I need to do something about organizing my day."

Discuss your growth goal with your husband, family, or others whose opinion you value. See what these persons have to say about your desired outcome. Any growth goal requiring very much change in daily routines will need a lot of support from your family. Realize that your desire for change may be seen as a threat to others. They may fear what change in you might mean for them. For example, prioritizing your day's activities might mean you won't drop everything to iron your daughter's blouse. Or, setting aside an hour each day for your quiet time might mean asking your husband or oldest child to care for the baby at that time. How will your priorities meet with their approval, fit into their schedules, or upset familiar family routines? Take into account any family resistance to reaching your goal, and work out ways of overcoming these barriers.

**Making Goals Come True**

Goals become realities by taking some steps to reach them. Finding out what steps to take is easy. Ask yourself: "What specific things must I do in order to reach my goal?" Several points need to be touched on in answering your question:

*1. Obstacles.*—What barriers will you have to overcome in reaching your goal? What attitudes do you have that might prevent moving toward your goal? What resistance might others have to your goal? What can you do to lessen or remove these barriers in the way of reaching your goal?

*2. Resources.*—What will be needed in reaching your goal? How much time, money, energy, skill, equipment, and the like will be required? How many of these resources do you have now or can you easily obtain? Where can you get help in getting needed resources? What resources can your husband, family, church, friends, community, or denomination provide?

*3. Support.*—Who can help you reach your growth goal? Who will give you encouragement or counsel? Who will hold you accountable in seeing that you work toward your goal? Who can give you feedback or insight into your progress? Who can you count on for pep talks or practical help?

*4. Starting helps.*—What specific things will you need to do in starting toward your goal? Do you need to gather information, learn new skills, assemble tools, or the like? Will you need to schedule time for study, travel, or activities?

Write down your responses to these four steps toward your goal. Once these steps are in place you can move toward your goal with the best possible chance of getting there. This approach to growth is focused and moves along practical lines. You can anticipate needs and obstacles, yet plan ways of overcoming them.

Set a time limit on your goal. Decide how much time will be needed to give your goal a chance of coming true. Check on your progress at regular intervals—daily, weekly, monthly, or as needed. You may find that some parts of your growth plans do not work or work less effectively than you'd like. You can then decide to drop or change these parts. For example, a plan to prioritize activities might be to make and follow a daily schedule for one month. At the end of the first week you might need to see if the schedule works out, if it seems too rigid, or if it failed to include needed items. Some small adjustments might be needed for the second week's schedule. At the month's end, you would need to see if your priorities were met in a better way. If so, build on that strength in planning for another month.

These steps of identifying a growth need, choosing a goal, coping with obstacles, gathering resources, finding support, planning growth steps, taking action, and evaluating progress can be applied to almost any kind of decision-making need you have. Simply decide where you are now and what you would like to see happen, and plan the steps to take you there.

Growth is something you decide to do. It doesn't happen by chance or automatically. You can choose to use change for the good it can bring. You can build on the reality of who you are and who you can become. You can reach toward your potential by understanding your needs and seeing them as growth points rather than dreading them. Redemptive growth is not an option for Christians but God's gift. Finding deeper meaning in life makes living productive and worthwhile. Your growth as a person affects those around you. You can help them choose growth in their own lives.

God reveals Himself in things, events, and people around you. His presence brings meaning to change. His purpose calls for your unique blend of traits, abilities, gifts, and personality. You are His child and Christ's gift to the church. These eternal truths are worth claiming and acting on in deciding where you want to go with your life.

## Enjoying Life's Seasons

Every season has its own beauty along with its hassles. The cold of winter lets the earth rest in preparation for new life in spring. The heat of summer speeds growth for autumn's harvest. Just as nature goes through cycles of change and growth, so you do. Childhood, youth, young adulthood, middle age, and older adulthood mark the years between birth and death. Marriage and career go through stages. Life has its seasons too.

Life's seasons can be less traumatic when

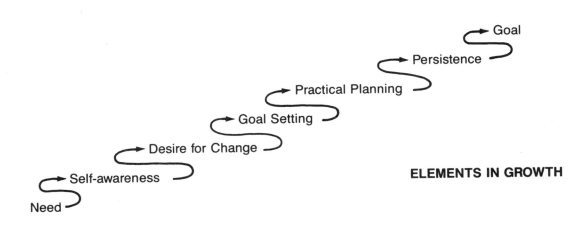

**ELEMENTS IN GROWTH**

Goal

Persistence

Practical Planning

Goal Setting

Desire for Change

Self-awareness

Need

you know what to expect. Read some books that describe the stages of marriage, career, and aging. These books usually discuss the changes and problems associated with each stage. Howard and Charlotte Clinebell deal with marriage stages in *The Intimate Marriage* (Harper and Row, 1970). Charles William Steward describes ministry stages in *Person and Profession: Career Development in the Ministry* (Abingdon, 1974). Gail Sheehy's *Passages* (Bantam Books, 1976) is a popular book about age development. Daniel G. Bagby looks at some of the major events in life and offers helps in dealing with them in *Transition and Newness* (Broadman, 1982). These and similar materials give some idea of what you'll face in your present life stage and what to expect in coming ones.

You can move more smoothly from one life stage to another by planning. Transition times seem unsettled and difficult. However, even these times can be faced with support from family, friends, spiritual mentors, and helping professionals. Any kind of change puts a strain on your sense of security. Being bumped out of a comfortable rut can be scary. The days before joy takes hold can be trying ones unless you have some sense of direction or pilgrimage in your life.

Working through life stages means centering on the spiritual values of your life. Keep in touch with your feelings; see how they are affecting your response to the life stage you are going through. Accept the encouragement of old friends, family members, and fellowship in the church. Renew your awareness of spiritual resources you can draw strength from: prayer, Bible reading, and worship. Give faith a chance to shape your view of the future. Take time to look at what God may be doing in your life now. You may be holding on to concepts that need updating. Concepts of God learned in childhood Sunday School class or adolescent struggles may need deepening to fit adult needs.

Aging seems to create dread in our youth-oriented society. Most products offer to keep users youthful. Looking at age seventy from a teen's viewpoint may indeed be shocking.

However, looking at that age from a sixty-nine-year-old's view is much less distressing. This author has found aging to be fulfilling and even comforting. Time's passing allows us to lay some responsibilities aside, to make peace with our youthful quests, and to enjoy the wisdom of experience.

Change gives you the opportunity to adjust your life, turn over a new page, and begin again. This hope is part of God's grace and blessing. Life's seasons can be times to reassess where you're going and what you want to do. All the children in school, the "empty nest," and retirement are examples of times to take a new look at your daily routine. The point is to take advantage of change in making life more satisfying.

### Growing As a Minister's Wife

Fulfillment as a minister's wife is something that must be learned but cannot be taught. Your unique blend of personality, experience, needs, and abilities sets the pace for your growth. These factors also largely determine your response to sharing life with a minister. How-to information can help you deal with major concerns and some minor irritations, but you will have to decide ways of balancing your public role with your private life. Only you have firsthand knowledge of what makes things work well in your situation. Start where you are, apply the ideas that seem most meaningful in your need, and see what happens. Here are some general strategies to consider:

• *Expectations.*—Think back to your first ideals about being a minister's wife. How well do you match those ideals now? Do you often wish you were not a minister's wife? If so, think of the things that trigger the wish. Perhaps you can locate a pattern of events or pressures that get you down. Check to see if your expectations of ministry are realistic. Someone may have promised you a bed of roses. What about expectations of yourself? Maybe you've demanded more of yourself than is necessary. Celebrate all the gifts you bring to your role, and value the support you give your husband.

• *Role pressures.*—Take advantage of fellowship with other ministers' wives. Ask how they feel about their role. Share problems and ways of coping. You'd be surprised what a relief it is to know you're not the only one feeling that way about problems! Attend seminars and retreats provided by your denomination that focus on your concerns.

Examine your successes and flops in serving as a minister's wife. What things make you feel most competent, and what makes you feel most vulnerable? Look for ways your strengths can balance less-than-optimum areas. List the things that make being a minister's wife the most interesting. What can you do to increase your list?

• *Time demands.*—Try reducing the number of events, activities, and leadership tasks you take on. List all the things you absolutely *must* do and put these in order by priority. Concentrate only on the top third of the list—the rest probably aren't that critical. Deal only with the first key items and temporarily set the others aside. Do these tasks first in the day or at the time you're at the peak of your strength. Once the very necessary items are cleared away, you'll probably feel less pressure in tending to the others.

Give yourself plenty of time to carry out tasks. Allow a little cushion of time for unexpected snags or surprises. Make a list of the things in your role as a minister's wife that make the most demands on your time. Do these items really merit all that time? When you know a particularly heavy schedule is coming up, be sure to build extra rest time into your day. Running yourself ragged will work only a short time before your body and mind rebel.

• *Fun and encouragement.*—Focus on the parts of being a minister's wife that you enjoy, that encourage you to go on, and that give you a lift. See how you might expand these areas. Accept all the encouragement you can get. Let others affirm your efforts in being a minister's wife.

Find some ways to feel release from routine. Choose a hobby, craft, or recreation you can do regularly just for the fun of it. Don't try to make a living off of needlework, for example, even if you love it—do it just for the sheer pleasure. Use this kind of activity for enjoyment more than accomplishment.

• *Renewal.*—Open your life to God's possibilities. God is greater than we know, far beyond the limits of our experience. He can bring hope and healing in ways you may not expect. Faith needs an ever-widening vision of God and His power: "that your minds may be opened to see his light, so that you will know what is the hope to which he has called you, how rich are the wonderful blessings he promises his people, and how very great is his power at work in us who believe. This power working in us is the same as the mighty strength which he used when he raised Christ from death and seated him at his right side in the heavenly world" (Eph. 1:18-20).

## Using Winning Ways

Competitiveness is a way of life today. A lot of emphasis goes to winning. People want to be on the winning side, root for the number one team, and admire success in every kind of activity. Being first almost takes on a fanatic quality in some individuals' lives. Many persons think that coming out on top justifies bending the rules and tilting the odds in their favor. A famous football coach suggested that winning is everything.

The New Testament, surprisingly enough, also talks about winning. But there are different standards for winning than our competitive culture might consider useful. Take the idea of the first being last or the greatest leader being the greatest servant of all, for example. Ministry embraces these sacred ideals of winning. Therefore, it's no wonder that ministry may bring you into conflict with some of the world's standards.

This book has sought to highlight some of the winning ways that fit into biblical ideals: understanding ministry and what people expect of leaders, affirming self, gaining relational skills, dealing with stress, responding to people in a caring way, dealing with life's tough tests, and choosing to grow as a person. These winning ways acknowledge both God's goodness as well as your own worth as His child. These winning ways accept the idea of a power greater than yourself who has a plan for this world and a purpose for you. Winning as a minister's wife, then, means being God's person as He created you to be.

What makes this kind of winning so different? For one thing, you don't have to prove anything to anyone, strive to be superior, put others down, or envy their abilities. Fulfilling God's purpose puts you way ahead of the game. A second difference lies in the prize you reach toward. God's prize is eternal, fulfilling, and deeply satisfying in a way earthly rewards barely touch on. Finally, your winning is not selfish—the more you fulfill God's purpose, the more you help others win.

The biblical idea of winning takes in the quality of being *winsome,* radiating a kind of charm based on joy, innocence, and inner grace. The writer James indicated that these traits came from spiritual wisdom: "wisdom from above is pure first of all; it is also peaceful, gentle, and friendly; it is full of compassion and produces a harvest of good deeds; it is free from prejudice and hypocrisy. And goodness is the harvest that is produced from the seeds the peacemakers plant in peace" (Jas. 3:17-18). Knowing and accepting yourself brings your worth as a person into focus. Opening your life to God's purpose affirms that worth through His indwelling Spirit. You can be winsome when you're free from the struggle to be someone you're not.

The apostle Peter described a special attractiveness that comes through being winsome rather than through expensive, artificial decorations: "Instead, your beauty should consist of your true inner self, the ageless beauty of a gentle and quiet spirit, which is of the greatest value in God's sight" (1 Pet. 3:4). There's nothing wrong with dressing nicely or looking attractive in an outward way, but there's a great deal wrong with using outward glamor as a substitute for self-esteem.

Winning ways won't take the tests and troubles out of your way, just make them endurable. Winning ways won't make your hassles any lighter, just make them bearable. Winning ways won't guarantee instant success in everything you do, just assure your welcome among all people of faith. Isn't that what victorious living really means—finding fulfillment in all you do, through good times and bad, through sorrows and celebrations, through the present into eternity.

### Time Out

List five small joys you've experienced today. How can you share these joys with your family?

How can your awareness of present joy help you prepare for your next task as a minister's wife?

*Recall the special times you've shared with your husband through his ministry, as though you were going to paint them as large murals for everyone to see. Let the shapes and colors of these times blend with the light of God:*

Dear Father, help me enjoy the colors of every day, the dark and the light, trusting in your plans for me as I grow as a person. Help me to see ministry as your garden of hope for our world, and as your gift for our lives as a family.

# For Further Reading

Bagby, Daniel G. *Transition and Newness* (Nashville: Broadman Press, 1982).

Blackburn, Bill. *Understanding Your Feelings* (Nashville: Broadman Press, 1983).

Baxter, Batsell Barrett. *When Life Tumbles In: Conquering Life's Problems* (Grand Rapids: Baker Book House, 1974).

Clinebell, Howard J. and Charlotte. *The Intimate Marriage* (New York: Harper and Row, 1970).

Coble, Betty J. *The Private Life of the Minister's Wife* (Nashville: Broadman Press, 1981).

Collins, Gary. *How to Be a People Helper* (Santa Ana, California: Vision House Publishers, 1976).

Dale, Robert D. *Surviving Difficult Church Members* (Nashville: Abingdon Press, 1984).

Drakeford, John W. *Do You Hear Me, Honey?* (New York: Harper and Row, 1976).

Faulkner, Brooks R. *Stress in the Life of the Minister* (Nashville: Convention Press, 1981).

Greenfield, Guy. *The Wounded Parent* (Grand Rapids: Baker Book House, 1982).

Hudson, R. Lofton. *Is This Divorce Really Necessary?* (Nashville: Broadman Press, 1983).

Ishee, John A. *From Here to Maturity* (Nashville: Broadman Press, 1975).

McSwain, Larry L., and William C. Treadwell, Jr. *Conflict Ministry in the Church* (Nashville: Broadman Press, 1981).

Mace, David and Vera. *What's Happening to Clergy Marriages?* (Nashville: Abingdon Press, 1980).

Madden, Myron C. *The Power to Bless: Healing and Wholeness Through Understanding* (Nashville: Broadman Press, 1970).

Montgomery, Felix E. *Pursuing God's Call: Choosing a Vocation in Ministry* (Nashville: Convention Press, 1981).

Montgomery, Shirley E. *A Growth Guide for Ministers' Wives* (Nashville: Broadman Press, 1984).

Oates, Wayne E. *Your Particular Grief* (Philadelphia: The Westminster Press, 1981).

Osborne, Cecil G. *Self-Esteem: Overcoming Inferiority Feelings* (Nashville: Abingdon Press, 1986).

Palmer, Stuart. *Role Stress* (Englewood Cliffs: Prentice-Hall, Inc., 1981).

Ross, Charlotte. *Who Is the Minister's Wife?* (Philadelphia: The Westminster Press, 1980).

Shostrom, Everett L., and Dan Montgomery. *God in Your Personality* (Nashville: Abingdon Press, 1986).

Sinclair, Donna. *The Pastor's Wife Today* (Nashville: Abingdon Press, 1981).

Westberg, Granger E. *Good Grief* (Philadelphia: Fortress Press, 1971).